seventeen ULTIMATE GUIDE TO STYLE

SEVENTEEN ULTIMATE GUIDE TO STYLE

Published by Running Press,
A Member of the Perseus Books Group

Books published by Running Press are available at special discounts
for bulk purchases in the United States by corporations,
institutions, and other organizations. For more information, please
contact the Special Markets Department at the Perseus Books Group,
2300 Chestnut Street, Suite 200, Philadelphia, PA 19103, or
call (800) 810-4145, ext. 5000, or e-mail special.markets@perseusbooks.com.

ISBN: 978-0-7624-4193-8
Library of Congress Control Number: 2011922744
E-book ISBN: 978-0-7624-4242-3

9 8 7 6 5 4 3 2 1

Number on the right indicates the number of this printing

Running Press Book Publishers
2300 Chestnut Street
Philadelphia, PA 19103-4371
Visit us on the web! www.runningpress.com

seventeen
ULTIMATE GUIDE TO
STYLE
HOW TO FIND YOUR PERFECT LOOK

ANN SHOKET
& THE EDITORS *of seventeen*

EDITED
by
JOANNA SALTZ

MELCHER
MEDIA

RUNNING PRESS
PHILADELPHIA · LONDON

NUMBER
SEVENTEEN,
NYC

Hi from Ann!

At *Seventeen,* it's our mission to make sure that you walk into every single situation with the **confidence** to own it. And a big part of finding that confidence is knowing that you look amazing. It's true—when you look good, you feel **great!**

We've highlighted six iconic style vibes in this book to help you find *your* perfect look. I love them all—probably because I've tried out each of them in my own way over the years! I had a **new wave/indie** moment with neon colors and geometric shapes. Then I went through my own **punk-rock rebellion** with shredded jeans and Doc Martens. There was a flannel-fueled grunge look that I'd rather forget. At the same time,

I've always had a fascination with glamorous **sky-high stilettos** and skin-tight minis. But underneath it all is a **classic** preppy girl who is happiest in rugby-striped polo shirts (with my collar popped!).

The idea that you can express yourself through clothes gives you an amazing sense of **freedom.** You can be **edgy** one day with a stack of spiked bracelets and a killer pair of boots, and then go **girly** the next with a soft chiffon dress (maybe paired with those killer boots for a cool twist!).

That's the best part of this book—there are no hard and fast fashion rules! You might fall madly **in love** with one style and match all the inspiration outfits. You could dip into one—or *all*—of the real girls' closets to get ideas. Or maybe you want to channel Selena Gomez for your **first day of school,** but then pick Rihanna as your style soul mate for holiday **parties!**

The whole point is that fashion is **crazy-delicious-insane fun** (or why else would you even want to get dressed?!?). There are tons of styling tricks, expert secrets, runway photos, and real-life street style in here to help you find the best look for **your** body and **your** style.

You're going to look great every single day—so get ready to own it!

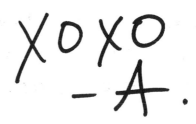

U
STYL

YOUR ULTIMATE GUIDE

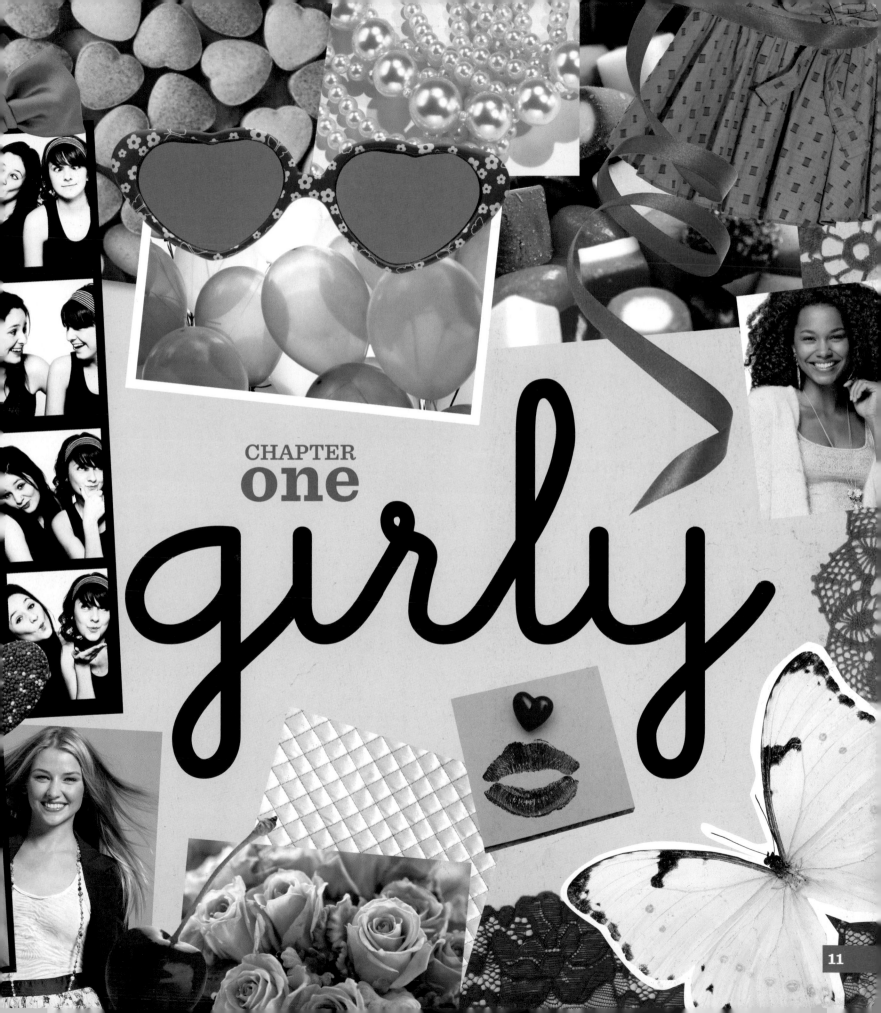

CHAPTER
one

girly

Girly style is all about striking the right balance between *sweet* and *sophisticated*. The secret is to look *pretty* without looking too perfect or prim. So get ready to play with fresh florals, swingy silhouettes, and flirty details like *ruffles* and *lace*. They'll all add up to a look that's a little sugar and a little spice.

girly MUST-HAVES

EIGHT ESSENTIAL PIECES

that'll instantly make any look a little cuter.

☑ FLORAL DRESS

Look for one in a **SOFT SHAPE**— you'll be able to layer just about anything over it.

☑ RUFFLED TOP

It's the kind of piece that works double duty: It's playful and **ADDS CUTE CURVES.**

☑ BALLET FLATS

Find ones with SPECIAL DETAILS, like quilting or bows, to give them more personality.

☑ PEEP-TOE HEELS

A BOLD COLOR makes these ultra-modern.

☑ BOOT-CUT JEANS

A LIGHT WASH goes perfectly with **PASTELS AND FLORALS.**

☑ SOFT TEE

love comes in different shades of red

A thin fabric and **A ROMANTIC SLOGAN** make an everyday top **FUN AND FEMININE.**

☑ CROPPED CARDIGAN

Your go-to piece when you want to **WARM UP A PRETTY DRESS.**

☑ FLOATY SKIRT

Just putting on something this flouncy and fun makes you **FEEL MORE FLIRTY.**

Turn your MUST-HAVES into these pretty looks.

what to wear with A FLORAL DRESS*

*

TINTED SHADES in a classic shape add a touch of glam.

A BRIGHT BELT highlights your waist.

AMAZING PLATFORMS keep a sweet dress from looking too dainty.

AN OVERSIZE COCKTAIL RING is just enough jewelry.

what to wear with A RUFFLED TOP*

Add a little sparkle to your look with **A CUTE RING** or two!

*

SLEEK, DARK JEANS transform a frilly top into a night-out look.

Ankle-length jeans are perfect for showing off **STUDDED, POINTY-TOE FLATS.**

what to wear with
BOOT-CUT JEANS*

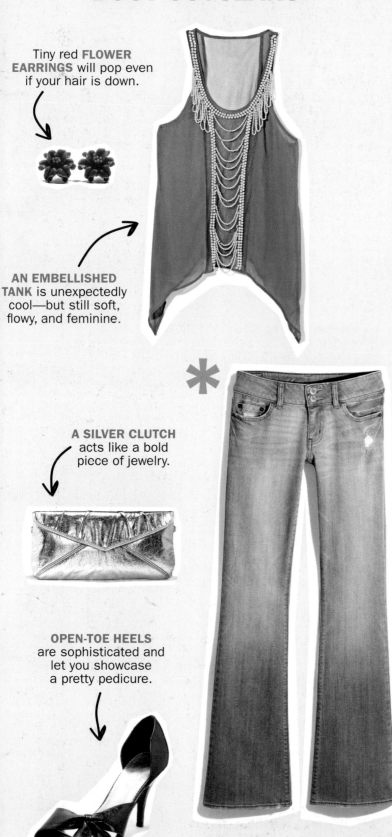

Tiny red **FLOWER EARRINGS** will pop even if your hair is down.

AN EMBELLISHED TANK is unexpectedly cool—but still soft, flowy, and feminine.

A SILVER CLUTCH acts like a bold piece of jewelry.

OPEN-TOE HEELS are sophisticated and let you showcase a pretty pedicure.

what to wear with
A CROPPED CARDIGAN*

A BRIGHT PRINTED SCARF adds a dose of personality.

A BIG CUFF gives the look a rock twist.

A PEPLUM SKIRT creates some flirty curves.

JEWELED BALLET FLATS make the outfit extra-special.

what to wear with BALLET FLATS*

Layer textures like **A GAUZY SCARF** and a **CHUNKY KNIT BERET** to create visual interest.

A LOOSE MINIDRESS shows off your legs (but with flats and a cardi, you won't look too exposed).

A CHARM BRACELET adds a vintage-y touch.

A STRUCTURED BAG with statement hardware is a classic!

what to wear with PEEP-TOE HEELS*

LONG, DANGLING EARRINGS draw the eye up to your pretty face!

Bright shoes call for **A BAG** in a complementary (not matchy-matchy!) color.

A WIDE BELT highlights your waist and gives shape to a full skirt.

THE FLORAL PRINT is girly, but the colors add a bold edge.

what to wear with
A SOFT TEE*

These **CLASSIC SUNNIES** give the look a cool feel.

BROKEN-IN DENIM SHORTS feel as comfy as sweats but look so much cuter!

Vibrant flowers make **A TOTE** casual enough for the beach, but metallic accents are perfect for a night on the boardwalk.

BARELY THERE SANDALS elongate your legs so you look nice and tall.

what to wear with
A FLOATY SKIRT*

Pair **A HOODIE** with **A TAILORED BUTTON-DOWN** so you don't look too casual.

COLORFUL BEADS add eye-catching drama.

When your outfit is tailored, **AN ARTSY BAG** makes it feel a little more fun.

Boy meets girl in a flirty way when you mix in **CUTE KICKS.**

girly girl
SHALYN

AGE
19

HOMETOWN
Bethlehem, PA

STAR SIGN
Aquarius

HOBBIES
Acting, writing,
boating, traveling

FAVE COLOR
Pink

"I'm a *girly* girl, but I never want to look too put together, so **I'LL ALWAYS MIX IN ONE OR TWO VINTAGE FINDS.**"

MY FAVORITE MOVIE MOMENT

"The costumes in *Marie Antoinette* were fantastic! To make my straight dresses poofier, I'll layer a colored tulle skirt underneath."

MY DESIGNER CRUSH

"Betsey Johnson is the ultimate girly designer. Sequins, candy colors, belted silhouettes—I always walk out of her store with something great."

my inspirations

MY STYLE SOUL MATE

"Aria from *Pretty Little Liars* dresses just like me! Her outfits—girly dresses with edgy accessories—always look unique, sweet, and fun without going overboard."

MY FAVORITE FASHION CITY

"I totally fell for the street style in London. It's the perfect mix of New York's all-out glam and the fancy couture of Paris. My favorite look? Girls in pantsuits with high heels."

ON THE STREET, LONDON, UK

MY GUILTY PLEASURE

"I've seen *Wicked* on Broadway five times! The costumes are so beautiful. Every time I go, something new stands out."

MY GO-TO PIECE

"Nobody makes oxfords as cool as Jeffrey Campbell does. I wear them with colored or lace tights to show off their pretty details."

{ my favorite looks }

school

"I like to update the standard jeans and tee look for school. And these **little flats** are great for running around campus all day— I always **roll up my jeans** to show them off."

date

"I want to look cute but not like I'm trying too hard. **Ruffles and a bright headband** are super-flirty, but the **denim jacket** helps tone it all down."

weekend

"When I'm grabbing sushi with friends, I like to play around with my style. My **laid-back chambray shirt** and **wedge sandals** make a **flirty skirt** feel completely original."

party

"The **bubble shape** and the **big bow** make this so **feminine and fun.** I'm known for throwing tea parties, and this would be the sweetest little hostess dress."

girly celeb-spiration

TAYLOR SWIFT

"I've always stuck to what I really like to wear, and that's *girly* things, dresses, and sparkle." —*Taylor*

insider secrets to getting
TAYLOR'S STYLE

one

Taylor loves to make her outfits special with one-of-a-kind touches like a piece of antique jewelry or fun patterned tights. **Choose just one strong piece to make a statement!**

two

When in doubt, pick a dress! Taylor's go-to piece looks as good with flats and a chic bag as it does with her roughed-up cowboy boots.

three

Don't be afraid of sparkle! Whether Taylor is going to a party or shopping with her mom, she loves to add a dash of sequins to her femme look.

four

A belt is a girl's best friend! To flaunt her flirty, feminine shape, Taylor tops off her dresses with skinny belts and wears wide, low-slung belts over jeans and tunics.

five

Surprise people with color! You'd think a girly-girl like Taylor would stick to just pastels, but every once in a while, she wows 'em with a hit of acid yellow or vivid purple!

taylor's
BEST GIRLY LOOKS

A drawstring waist adds some cute curves to a flowy peasant dress.

A soft pink dress with pleats and daring cutouts is a modern take on the ballerina trend.

A little black mini is ultra-feminine in sparkly black lace.

Girly gets an indie twist when you take a retro-floral dress and add fun blue shoes!

A blousy top and faded cutoffs are the perfect summer uniform.

A bright yellow dress alone makes a sunny statement.

A loose blouse in creamy white has a soft, angelic appeal (even with knee-high boots!).

Graphic stripes paired with strong red have a chic Parisian feel.

girly STYLING TRICKS TO TRY

You don't need a personal stylist to look amazing. **CHECK OUT THESE TIPS** for getting girly just right.

MIX YOUR FLORALS!

Matching prints doesn't have to be daunting. Just offset a larger pattern with a smaller one **IN THE SAME COLOR PALETTE.**

PILE ON YOUR NECKLACES!

STACK TWO OR THREE of your favorite pendants. Make sure they fall at different lengths so they don't overlap.

PICK THE RIGHT CARDI!

USE A CARDI TO CREATE AN ULTRA-FEMININE SHAPE. It's all about proportion: Pair a flowy one that hits at your hip or lower with a sleek pencil skirt or skinny jeans. Or try a more form-fitting sweater with a full swingy skirt.

ACCESSORIZE YOUR **HAIR!**

GIVE YOUR JEWELRY BOX A REST and dress up your hair instead. A big bow clip, flirty feather headband, or bright floral hair tie can be just as cute as a necklace and earrings.

JUST ADD **HEELS!**

PAIR YOUR JEANS WITH YOUR FAVORITE HEELS to make your legs look like they never end. The hem should hit halfway down the heel and rest just above your toes.

WINTERIZE YOUR **SUMMER DRESS!**

ALL IT TAKES IS SOME LAYERING MAGIC— add a long-sleeved shirt underneath and a thin sweater on top to give the whole look polish. Leggings make any dress or skirt work in cooler seasons.

your girly LOOK BOOK

These chic looks straight off the runway, the red carpet, *and* the street will give you endless style ideas!

CHARLOTTE RONSON

A bold floral gets a trendy camp vibe when paired with a tackle vest and slouchy socks.

ZOË SALDANA

Ground a poufy party dress with a cropped black jacket.

NEW YORK CITY

A tiered floral skirt can feel almost too princess-y—so give it some sophistication with a solid black sleeveless turtleneck.

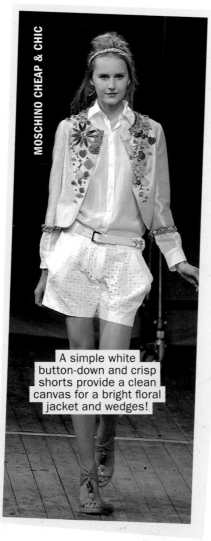

MOSCHINO CHEAP & CHIC

A simple white button-down and crisp shorts provide a clean canvas for a bright floral jacket and wedges!

CAMILLA BELLE

Use accessories to give your girly look some attitude—the red belt and hoops have a glam feel.

NINA RICCI

Pretty ruffles on a skirt and heels are timeless and romantic.

Play up the artsy vibe of a vintage oversize-floral dress with a knit cap and lace-up ankle booties.

OLIVIA PALERMO

A big pattern becomes even more fun with a contrasting belt and a bold bag.

LAUREN CONRAD

When the silhouette of your dress is so sweet, look for a cool print to amp things up.

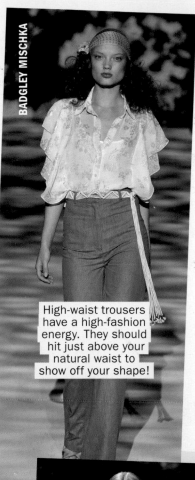

BADGLEY MISCHKA

High-waist trousers have a high-fashion energy. They should hit just above your natural waist to show off your shape!

LUCA LUCA

Subtle *can* be sexy. A pencil skirt lets you flaunt your waist and hips.

NEW YORK CITY

Black-and-white pearls reinvent the classic necklace, but it's the vibrant color of the dress that adds life to the look.

BLAKE LIVELY

A super-strong print won't feel overpowering if you keep accessories minimal.

D&G

Two loud florals can work great together if they both have uncomplicated silhouettes.

SHOP *girly*

Hit these go-to spots for all your girly gear!

betsey johnson

Known for her playful use of tulle, bows, sparkle, and bright floral prints, Betsey Johnson is the queen of girly designers.

lulu's

With flirty rompers, cropped jackets, sweet bags, and jewelry, you can create an adorable head-to-toe look at lulu.com's online shop.

victoria's secret pink

This line is known for its cute panties and ultra-flattering bras, as well as its cozy loungewear must-haves, like soft tees and leggings.

charlotte russe

Always on top of the latest trends, this fun store has everything from lacy tops to delicate scarves and pretty jewelry.

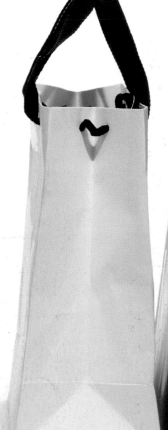

bp at nordstrom

Stock up on cute tees, tanks, and sweaters in all different colors in the juniors section of Nordstrom department store.

windsor

Scope out racks and racks of party dresses to find the perfect option for prom, Sweet Sixteen, homecoming, and more!

express

Got a big date? Make this mall staple your first stop for Saturday night outfits that have a sexy vibe.

delia's

Cute jeans and tees, little black dresses, and bright coats come in extended sizes, so they'll fit every body type!

CHAPTER
two

edgy

twilight

Nothing will be the same.

Get the **edgy** look by channeling your inner **rock star** and turning up the volume on your style. Rip up your jeans, **rough** up your leather, and add a kick of studs and chains. But the real secret to getting this look right is in the **mix:** Add feminine touches—layered bangles, a peek of lace—to soften the effect. You'll look **amped** up in all the right places.

edgy
MUST-HAVES
EIGHT ESSENTIAL PIECES
to spark up any outfit.

☑ **SKINNY JEANS**

Look for details like zippers at the bottom, which **ADD A TOUGH EDGE.**

☑ TUNIC TOP

A slouchy tunic gives off an **"I JUST THREW THIS ON"** vibe—in a good way!

Strong shoes like these can **MAKE YOUR WHOLE OUTFIT COOLER!**

☑ BOOTIES

☑ ROCK TEE

Old-school T-shirts are packed with personality and can be **GREAT CONVERSATION STARTERS.**

☑ BLACK MINI

STEP UP YOUR STYLE in a teeny mini. A flashy skirt should hit four inches above the knee.

☑ LEATHER BOMBER

It gives any look—a plain tee, a floral dress— **INSTANT ATTITUDE.**

☑ MOTORCYCLE BOOTS

Your go-to accessory— they take even your most basic pieces to **A ROCK PLACE.**

Try these year-round—they're so much **MORE DARING THAN A DENIM MINI.**

☑ DENIM CUTOFFS

35

Take your MUST-HAVES to the edge with these fierce fashion ideas.

what to wear with SKINNY JEANS*

SAILOR STRIPES AND LACE APPLIQUÉS soften tough-girl jeans.

A STUDDED CLUTCH is a glitzy surprise!

A STAR RING is a cool hit of bling.

COLORED METALLIC HEELS add a playful touch.

what to wear with A ROCK TEE*

ONE UNIQUE NECKLACE that shows your individual taste is nice. Two of them are twice as awesome!

A LACE SKIRT is the perfect counterpoint to a vintage tee.

A striped **MESSENGER BAG** adds some cool texture.

These **LACE-UP BOOTS** add just enough ruggedness.

what to wear with
BOOTIES*

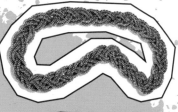

A WOVEN CHAIN NECKLACE is such a major statement that you don't need earrings.

A SKULL BAUBLE shows you're wild, but in a fun way.

A FLIRTY DRESS in a loud print is the perfect centerpiece.

A LADYLIKE BAG (with a rock detail like studs) is fancy without being too stuffy.

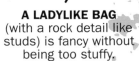
*

what to wear with
A TUNIC TOP*

*

Show fashion creativity with a **SNAKESKIN-PRINT BAG.**

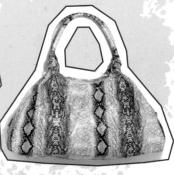

GRAY SKINNIES with subtle whiskering are more fun than basic leggings.

STACKED BANGLES are a must—mixing styles and colors makes a graphic impact.

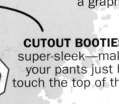

CUTOUT BOOTIES look super-sleek—make sure your pants just barely touch the top of the shoe.

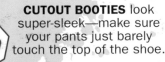

what to wear with
A LEATHER BOMBER *

Give a bomber a personal touch by topping it with **A STUDDED SCARF.**

A SILVER TOTE BAG really pops against a black-and-red backdrop.

Rock **ONE REALLY COLORFUL PIECE**—it's a fun touch to an all-black outfit.

LACE-FREE GRAPHIC TENNIS SHOES are low maintenance and high intensity at the same time.

what to wear with
A BLACK MINI *

Bad hair day? Who cares! **A FEDORA** is a fast and trendy fix.

A PRINTED SCARF can instantly tie an entire look together when you're rushing to get out the door.

A leather mini can work for class when you pair it with **A COMFY SWEATSHIRT.**

A CLASSIC BOWLER BAG looks so much cooler with a metallic kick.

COLORFUL KICKS keep the look casual but cool.

what to wear with DENIM CUTOFFS*

what to wear with MOTORCYCLE BOOTS*

ZEBRA PRINT AND STRIPES layered together under an **ARMY-STYLE JACKET** makes for a quirky-fun look.

A PLAID BUTTON-DOWN gives your style a preppy twist.

WINGED EARRINGS offer an angelic touch.

TASSELS, STUDS, AND CHAINS can live in harmony on one piece—but keep the rest of your accessories much less flashy.

GRAY WORKS AS A NEUTRAL, but the studs keep it from being boring.

DARK LEGGINGS let your boots take center stage.

edgy girl
NICOLE

AGE
21

HOMETOWN
New York, NY

STAR SIGN
Cancer

HOBBIES
Traveling, reading, dancing
with friends, listening to music

FAVE COLOR
Purple

"I'm all about chill,
laid-back clothes, but
**I LIKE TO
ADD SOME EDGE**
with **tough** or wild accessories."

MY BEAUTY OBSESSION

"Instead of the typical black polish, I go for more unusual colors like dark purple or green. It still looks edgy but adds a more sophisticated touch."

MY FAVORITE FASHION CITY

"I feel most connected to Tokyo. The street fashion, the shopping, and the overall energy of the city really resonate with my personal style."

MY GO-TO PIECE

"A leather jacket makes everything from jeans to dresses go from dull to exciting."

my inspirations

MY DESIGNER CRUSH

"Patricia Field is totally out there, sexy, and fun. She knows how to add life to her clothes with unexpected details like oversize ruffles, wild prints, or big zippers."

MY STYLE SOUL MATE

"Gwen Stefani isn't afraid to try different things with her music *or* her style. I think she embodies the edgy spirit, and I'm always excited to see what she'll wear next."

MY ACCESSORY OBSESSION

"Leopard prints, skulls, metallics—I have a huge collection of scarves in bright colors and cool prints."

my favorite looks

party

"My favorite time to take fashion risks is when I'm at a concert or a club. **Playful accessories** like knee-highs and a sparkly necklace let me show off my bold style."

school

"I like to dress to impress when I have a class presentation. A **denim vest cools up a feminine dress,** and sleek heels and bold bangles give it polish."

date

"A leather mini and extra-long earrings **are drop-dead sexy,** but a sleeveless hoodie and mesh top add that down-to-earth vibe—it's perfect for meeting people."

weekend

"Comfort is key for me, but I never want to look messy. Cool gold necklaces and motorcycle boots **make the outfit** with my worn-in jeans and faded rock tee."

edgy celeb-spiration
ASHLEY TISDALE

"I love how a short dress can go really **edgy** just by putting a leather jacket on. I like things you can wear again in a different way." —*Ashley*

insider secrets to getting
ASHLEY'S STYLE

1

Embrace your dark side!
For some girls, head-to-toe black can look gloomy. But Ashley mixes textures and always lets a peek of skin show, so her look is sleek, not scary!

2

Forget perfection!
Unlace your boots, pick shredded jeans, or wear a mismatched pile of chains! Ashley knows that those sorts of details make *every* look more interesting.

3

Love the leather!
Ashley slips into a sleek jacket or hot mini whenever she wants to feel sexy and tough.

4

Add some flash!
Ash loves to glam up her style with a head-turning accent, like a studded belt or bold bag.

5

Give your look the boot!
Chunky moto boots or stiletto booties are Ashley's go-to accessory—for her, the rougher, the better.

ashley's
BEST EDGY LOOKS

Leather leggings and an oversize rock tee—the ultimate edgy uniform.

Even a floral print can walk the edge—a leather jacket and chain-strap bag take it there.

Rough up a cargo jacket with acid-wash jeans and open-toe boots.

A soft, worn-in tee is a cool contrast to a tough leather jacket and distressed jeans.

A slinky minidress goes from sexy to fierce with a studded belt and awesome shoes.

Chunky booties and a knit jacket help balance out a loose tank dress.

Steel gray makes a simple dress cool and sophisticated.

A basic tee and cutoffs get a rock touch with studded accents and black shades!

edgy
STYLING TRICKS TO TRY

**Pull off the rocker look—your way.
Try one of these AMAZING SECRETS.**

STEP UP YOUR SWEATS!

Nothing gives your wardrobe an "I don't care" feel like sweats. But to keep them feeling chic— not sloppy—pair them with structured pieces **LIKE A FITTED MINI OR SLIM PANTS.**

ADD A TANK OVER A TEE!

Lazy-day clothes get a cool update when you layer an eye-catching tank on top. **IT SHOWS OFF YOUR SHAPE WITHOUT SHOWING SKIN!**

DESTROY YOUR BOOTS!

Scuffing your new boots gives them a cool vintage vibe. Get that worn-in look by quickly **HAMMERING ACROSS THE LEATHER** or by using a fine-grade sandpaper to take down the shine!

LAYER YOUR BANGLES!

Stacked bracelets are a fun way to show your punky side. **THE KEY IS TO MIX STYLES** too—a super-sparkly bangle can play off a lacquered black bracelet in a fun way.

WARM UP YOUR CUTOFFS!

SLASH YOUR LEGGINGS!

TIGHTS AND BOOTS TRANSITION THEM THROUGH THE SEASONS and give your winter look some texture.

Make a big impact by creating slits in your leggings. Pick random spots and puncture them with the end of a safety pin to control the cut. **MAKE SURE YOU SPACE SLASHES AT LEAST TWO INCHES APART** to avoid creating a gaping hole!

your edgy
LOOK BOOK

Add some heat to your wardrobe with these inspirations straight off the runway, the red carpet, *and* the street.

MIRANDA COSGROVE

Even an edgy chick can show her girly side— a super-full metallic skirt is a chic counterpoint to a shearling bomber, chains, and lace-up booties.

BALMAIN

Frayed teeny shorts don't feel sloppy when you inject a pop of glam, like a sparkly jacket.

L.A.M.B.

KRISTEN STEWART

A drapey tunic softens ultra-tight black leggings and cutout heels.

A minidress looks extra-daring in bold black and electric blue. The open shoes make it feel like a *look*, not just a dress!

NEW YORK CITY

Patterned tights are a fun alternative to fishnets and lace.

BALENCIAGA

Flash your fashion confidence—wear a tank under a sheer, patterned buttoned-up blouse and top it with an edgy cardi.

LOS ANGELES

Studs instantly toughen a dress, but the open back keeps it looking flirty.

NEW YORK CITY

An edgy fashion risk that works: denim on denim pulled together with a tee and black tights.

DIESEL

Go '80s with an off-the-shoulder sweatshirt. It's punk pretty with a flirty skirt and intense boots.

TAYLOR MOMSEN

Make sexy, over-the-knee boots the standout part of your outfit. Keep the rest of your look low-key.

ISABEL MARANT

A buffalo plaid shirt and slouchy black boots are perfect with ragged cutoffs.

NEW YORK CITY

In black, a lace top goes from sweet to sexy!

MILEY CYRUS

A minidress with long sleeves is so much cooler and lets your legs take center stage.

NEW YORK CITY

With destroyed jeans, all you need is a simple slouchy top.

51

SHOP edgy

Hit these go-to spots for all your rock pieces!

topshop

Take inspiration from London street style! This cool British retailer has a store in NYC, or shop at topshop.com to bring the best UK fashions to your town.

dr. martens

This shoe company has been around since the '60s, so no one knows authentic punk better. Its boots add tough appeal to any look.

h+m

A fashionista's fave for great runway-inspired bargains. You can even find major designers at affordable prices.

diesel

Express your fashion-forward side with these Italian-made jeans—they'll be the pair you throw on again and again.

steve madden

We dare you not to find a boot you absolutely love here! Besides its impressive selection, Steve Madden often has the latest runway-inspired styles before anyone else.

girl props

This online store is your one-stop shop for funky jewelry. Grab a skull necklace or a blinged-out initial ring (or both!)—most of its stuff is $10 or less!

hot topic

Stock up on graphic tees and novelty printed tops at this mall staple. You'll be surprised by its wide selection of lacy tights and fishnets too.

alloy

Alloy.com has jeans galore! Find the right boot-cut, skinny, and destroyed denim to flatter your body, and top with a cool embellished tunic from the huge selection.

CHAR
LOTT
E RO
NSON

CHAPTER three
boho

The **boho** girl is a *free spirit*—with a *carefree* style to match. It's all about layering patterns and fun details to give you that overall *earthy* feel: Start with a little floral, pile on some suede, add something fringed, and top it all off with soft knits and tons of beads. It's where *high fashion* meets low-key.

boho
MUST-HAVES

to give you the ultimate boho-chic style.

☑ PAISLEY DRESS

A FREE-FLOATING DRESS looks amazing on every body type—but keep accessories subtle so they won't compete with a busy print.

☑ FLOWY TOP

Choose a breezy shirt with **GIRLY DETAILS** (like crochet) to play up the feminine factor.

☑ MESSENGER BAG

A cross-body bag has that "just threw this on" vibe, especially in **BROKEN-IN LEATHER.**

☑ MAXISKIRT

Maxiskirts feel how they look— **DRAPEY AND CASUAL,** but still pretty and light.

☑ DESTROYED DENIM

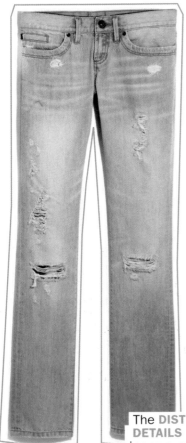

The **DISTRESSED DETAILS** give your jeans a cool edge.

☑ MILITARY JACKET

A military jacket gives any outfit some structure, but in **A RELAXED WAY.**

☑ GLADIATOR SANDALS

They have a **NATURAL APPEAL**—like one style step above being barefoot.

☑ LONG CARDIGAN

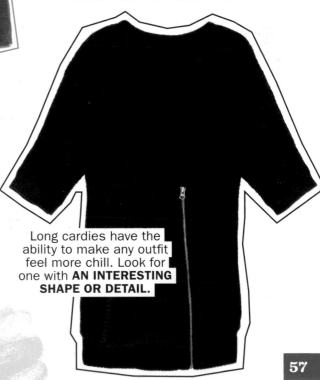

Long cardies have the ability to make any outfit feel more chill. Look for one with **AN INTERESTING SHAPE OR DETAIL.**

Use your MUST-HAVES to create a look that's soft, pretty, and playful.

what to wear with A PAISLEY DRESS*

OVERSIZE SUNGLASSES add a touch of movie-star attitude.

*

Your jewelry shouldn't battle your outfit for attention. **ONE CUFF** and a fab **COCKTAIL RING** should do the trick.

EDGIER HEELS make the look more sophisticated.

what to wear with A FLOWY TOP*

*

Draw the eye to a pretty neckline with **A BEADED NECKLACE.**

SLIM-FITTING JEANS are a sleek accompaniment to a more voluminous top.

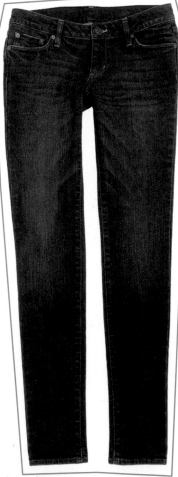

A SLOUCHY LEATHER BAG gives a simple outfit some personality.

MOCCASIN FLATS have a Southwest kick, and suede makes them oh-so-cozy.

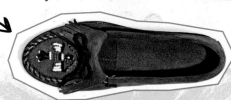

what to wear with
A MESSENGER BAG*

TEENY FLORAL EARRINGS give your look a subtle hit of sparkle.

Add **A LIGHT SWEATER** and scarves to keep warm on a breezy day. Then give the look more shape by strapping your messenger bag across your body.

Scrunch down bright socks and no one will overlook your **GREAT BOOTS.**

what to wear with
A MAXISKIRT*

With such a basic top, **GLAM EARRINGS** add a little sparkle to your upper half.

A FITTED TANK offsets the loose skirt so your body doesn't get lost in your outfit.

A BIG STONE RING looks glam in a cool, accidental way.

A maxiskirt begs for **WEDGE SHOES**—they peek out from underneath and keep your hem from dragging on the floor!

what to wear with
DESTROYED DENIM*

A **SWEET CAPELET** provides structure—but over a tee, it still feels casual.

Since rips and holes have a lived-in feeling, dress things up with **DANGLING BEADED EARRINGS.**

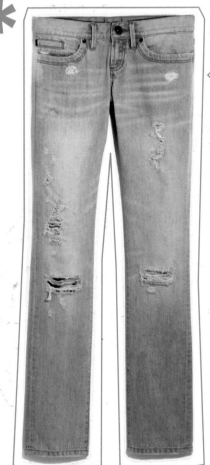

*

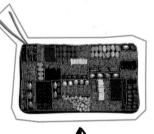

Make your entire outfit feel more exotic with a **COLORFUL BEADED CLUTCH.**

SIMPLE STRAPPY SANDALS are all you need when the rest of your outfit has so much going on.

what to wear with
A MILITARY JACKET*

*

A **SIMPLE WOODEN PENDANT** adds a feminine touch to the jacket's structured neckline!

Check your local thrift shops for **ARTSY BRACELETS.**

Ease the jacket's ruggedness with **PASTEL PRINTED JEANS.**

DOWN-TO-EARTH SHOES make the whole look ultra-mellow.

what to wear with
GLADIATOR SANDALS*

Balance the laid-back vibe of denim shorts and casual sandals with a **PRETTY FLORAL BLOUSE.**

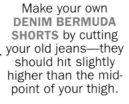

Make your own **DENIM BERMUDA SHORTS** by cutting your old jeans—they should hit slightly higher than the midpoint of your thigh.

When wearing a busy print, select a **PURSE IN A SOLID COLOR** and rich texture—like suede—so it pops but doesn't clash with your top.

*

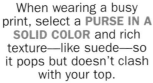

what to wear with
A LONG CARDIGAN*

*

A CHUNKY, ANGLED NECKLACE plays up the V-neck of a cardigan.

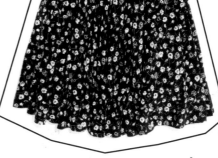

Pair a drapey cardi with a **FLIRTY MINI** for an extra dose of femininity!

A SLOUCHY BACKPACK toughs up the outfit so it doesn't feel too precious.

JEWELED SANDALS embellished with pretty stones are like jewelry for your feet!

boho girl
ANDIE

AGE
20

HOMETOWN
Montclair, NJ

STAR SIGN
Capricorn

HOBBIES
Arts and crafts, running,
watching old movies

FAVE COLOR
Green

"My look may change from day to day, but **THERE'S ALWAYS THIS UNDERLYING QUIRKY,** grungy, bohemian vibe."

MY BEAUTY OBSESSION

"Girls with really long hair always look amazing. Hair can make or break an outfit, and when you're going for a certain vibe like boho, I think it adds a lot to your look."

BLAKE LIVELY

MY CRAFTY PASSION

"Handmade jewelry like friendship bracelets or beaded necklaces adds major personality to any look. I love creating my own unique pieces with rope, string, charms, or beads."

MY GO-TO ACCESSORY

"I love wearing quirky socks with things they don't normally go with. Instead of just black tights and boots, I'll add bright knee socks too."

my inspirations

MY FAVORITE FOOTWEAR

"Clogs are incredible! They add that perfect earthy style to short dresses and tights, or cutoffs and chunky socks."

MY STYLE SOUL MATE

"I love how Mary-Kate Olsen's look feels laid-back and fashion-forward at the same time. She always stays true to her own style."

MY SHOPPING STRATEGY

"A lot of my favorite clothes come from thrift stores like the Salvation Army. I go as often as I can— and I head for the dresses first and then the men's flannel."

my favorite looks

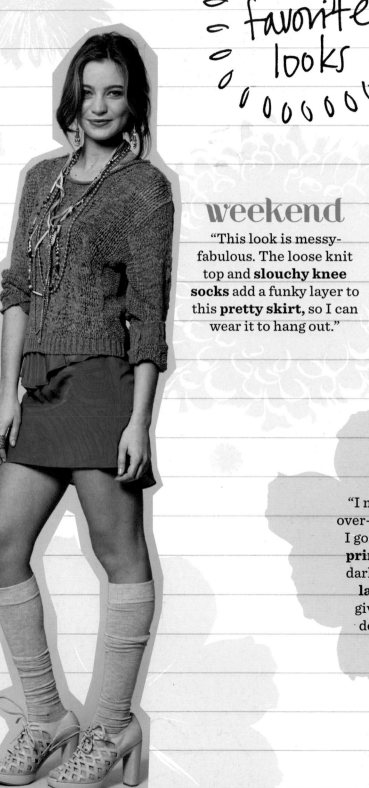

weekend

"This look is messy-fabulous. The loose knit top and **slouchy knee socks** add a funky layer to this **pretty skirt,** so I can wear it to hang out."

party

"I never want to feel over-the-top sexy when I go out. This **animal print** is bold, but the dark accessories and **layered jewelry** give it a laid-back, downtown vibe."

I ♥ mix

school

"Cutoffs are my favorite summer staple. **Dark tights** and **a longer top** make them more polished and appropriate for school."

date

"This is the **perfect dress** for a fancy lunch with my boyfriend on a sunny day. The bright colors are fun, but the **long, loose silhouette** makes it more casual."

boho celeb-spiration

VANESSA HUDGENS

"I'm so into the hippie bohemian thing. I love long flowy skirts. I love tousled hair. I love earth tones." —*Vanessa*

insider secrets to getting
VANESSA'S STYLE

one

Show your shape! On Vanessa's small frame, too many flowy, loose pieces would look overwhelming. So she always wears at least one fitted piece—a tank or skinny jeans—to look relaxed but not lost.

two

Get creative! A bohemian girl will always choose something handmade over something manufactured—and Vanessa is no exception. She loves to wear crafty jewelry, like oversize beads, that give her style a one-of-a-kind feel.

three

Embrace nature! Like a true California girl, Vanessa looks to nature for fashion inspiration. You'll always see her in soft fabrics and earthy tones, as well as feathers and shell beads.

four

Hold the heels! Vanessa doesn't like to teeter—she prefers chunky platforms or flat, strappy sandals to super-sexy stilettos. They keep her boho vibe going all the way down to her toes.

five

Sweeten things up! Lots of dark colors, leather, and wood worn together can look droopy—so she mixes in pops of girliness like something floral or sparkly.

67

vanessa's BEST BOHO LOOKS

Metallic shine adds
a luxe touch to an
earth-tone knit dress.

Channel a Greek
goddess in a flowy dress,
medallion necklace, and
fierce gladiator sandals.

Mix a ruffled vintage-y
tank with a relaxed
peasant skirt for
a soft, sweet look.

A dark belt breaks
up a busy print and
adds shape to
a loose maxidress.

Layered necklaces stand out against a cool blue mini.

Show off your flirty side in a fun romper with a bright floral print.

Suede boots and a fringed bag are a boho girl's best friends.

Transform a sweet denim dress with a hippie-ish floppy hat and strappy sandals.

boho
STYLING TRICKS TO TRY

Working that free-spirited style is easier than you think. Just try out these SIMPLE FASHION SECRETS and voilà!

TRANSFORM A DRESS!

LET THE PRINT OF A PRETTY DRESS PEEK OUT as a skirt when you layer a tee on top!

BELT YOUR BLOUSY STUFF!

A THICKER LEATHER BELT GIVES SHAPE TO A FREE-FLOWING DRESS— find one in a cool texture or bright color to instantly liven up a simple print.

GO TRIBAL!

LOOK FOR OVERSIZE BEADED NECKLACES that have a global feel! They give off that "I just picked this up during my travels" vibe and can make even the most basic outfit feel exotic and chic.

PERSONALIZE YOUR RIPPED DENIM!

Take your ripped jeans from basic to bold
by pinning a piece of lace underneath—
IT ADDS AN ELEMENT OF SURPRISE!

DRESS UP YOUR CARGOS!

A LOOSE, PRETTY TOP makes slim cargos
feel fashion-y. Throw on heels and glam earrings,
and suddenly you have a hot date look!

MAKE A STATEMENT WITH A COZY HAT!

Here's a hat trick for your wardrobe: Wear your chunky,
warm winter hat to top off a casual look. **IT'S AN
UNEXPECTEDLY COOL TOUCH.** (Step it up one more notch
by making a side braid or letting a messy side bun peek out.)

your boho
LOOK BOOK

Copy these mellow styles from the red carpet, the runway *and* the street—each has a special quality that nails that fashionable attitude.

CHARLOTTE RONSON

Socks under your sandals are the perfect boho touch to a flowy skirt.

ZOË KRAVITZ

Even all black gets a boho twist when you wear a tribal-inspired headband in just the right way.

ISABEL MARANT

Pair slouchy boots with a summer dress for California-cool style.

MISSONI

Accentuate a funky retro dress with a floppy hat and tie-dyed gladiator sandals.

HILARY DUFF

A loose romper and braided belt say a lot. Keep the rest simple with nude heels.

NEW YORK CITY

A Southwest-inspired jacket and skirt look modern paired with bold tights and high-heeled ankle booties.

LONDON

A boyfriend blazer adds some structure to a loose crocheted dress and fringed bag.

AUDRINA PATRIDGE

A strapless dress with colorful embroidery up top is an easy, all-in-one outfit.

PUCCI

Take boho to a rock level with paisley pants and tough accessories.

NEW YORK CITY

Wooden bracelets and thong sandals are the perfect accompaniments to an earth-toned top and shorts.

WHITNEY PORT

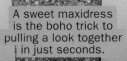

A sweet maxidress is the boho trick to pulling a look together in just seconds.

NANETTE LEPORE

Amp up dark skinny jeans with a beaded, tribal-influenced top.

SHENAE GRIMES

Modernize a prairie-inspired dress with a graphic cami underneath and trendy shoes.

NEW YORK CITY

A breezy tank makes skinny leggings feel laid-back—a bright bag adds a dose of color.

SHOP boho

Hit these go-to spots for all your earthy essentials!

pacsun

This store is known for its beachy apparel, but you'll find more than great-priced swimsuits. Scour the shelves for pretty tanks, animal-print dresses, and casually cute hoodies.

hollister

Dressing down is effortless with racks and racks of surfer-inspired looks. The clothes come in bold, colorful prints, so every day feels like a beach day.

roxy

This surfer-girl shop has you covered all year long: flirty, printed bikinis for the summer, cozy hoodies and T-shirts for layering in the winter.

lucky brand

The laid-back SoCal-influenced clothing here features cool prints like Liberty florals and plaids—plus tons of denim.

anthropologie

Its luxe boho pieces are worth the splurge! Shop flowy designer pieces or make a statement with earthy vintage jewelry.

alternative apparel

The Alternative Earth line at this eco-conscious retailer is made with organic cotton and recycled polyester, so you can look cute while making a global impact.

planet blue

Originally a boutique in Malibu, this boho store is a celeb fave. It's maintained its roots by featuring butterfly-wing tops as well as maxidresses, all available at planetblue.com.

swell

Swell.com has a surprising collection of chic, relaxed clothes ranging from items like metallic dresses to knit boots.

CHAPTER
four
classic

The **classic** style is **crisp** and **clean** forever and always—but never the least bit boring. Think understated lines and **simple silhouettes** like a sharp blazer or the perfect little black dress. Then go for preppy patterns and **playful** elements—like a cool stripe or a quilted bag. The end result is an amazing look that'll never go out of style.

CLASSIC
MUST-HAVES

EIGHT ESSENTIAL PIECES to make your timeless look totally modern.

☑ **OXFORD SHIRT**

A collared button-down adds the ultimate **PREPPY TOUCH** to every outfit.

☑ RIDING BOOTS

Slip these on with any outfit to give your look a **COOL EQUESTRIAN VIBE.**

☑ STRIPED BLAZER

A great way to make your outfit instantly **MORE POLISHED.**

☑ QUILTED PURSE

The perfect piece— **TRENDY YET TIMELESS.**

☑ A-LINE SKIRT

It's a **FLIRTY SHAPE** that flatters every body.

☑ LITTLE BLACK DRESS

This staple can take you **FROM A DANCE TO A DATE** (and even to school)!

☑ BOOT-CUT JEANS

This **SLEEK SHAPE** is a wardrobe workhorse—the classy alternative to skinnies you'll wear with everything!

☑ MARY-JANE HEELS

Sweet meets sexy—**WEAR THEM WITH YOUR FAVORITE JEANS** for a fun going-out look.

Here's how to wear your MUST-HAVES in the most stylish way.

WHAT TO WEAR WITH AN OXFORD SHIRT*

READING GLASSES have a studious feel (even if you don't need them!).

A polished shirt cries out for **ROUGHED-UP JEANS.**

A LONG-HANDLE BAG looks neat but still trendy.

HIGH HEELS glam up a casual look.

WHAT TO WEAR WITH RIDING BOOTS*

CHARM BRACELETS and **PEARLS** are old-school classics.

Leave a few buttons undone so **A POLO SWEATER** doesn't feel so prim.

A DENIM MINISKIRT should land about three inches above your knee—short enough to be cute and long enough to be appropriate everywhere!

what to wear with
A LITTLE BLACK DRESS*

A STATEMENT NECKLACE that mixes rhinestones and soft petals is pretty but not super-dainty.

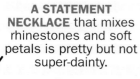

A GLITTERING BRACELET is an easy way to add major glamour.

Delicate ruching transforms **A CLUTCH** from simple to special.

Feel extra-sexy in your LBD by wearing it with **FLASHY HEELS.**

what to wear with
A STRIPED BLAZER*

A STRIPED DRESS works under a striped blazer if the stripes are different widths.

Layering your favorite **CHAINS AND CHARMS** gives the look a personal touch.

METALLIC FLATS are dressy without the "ouch!" of sky-high heels.

Add a burst of color with a **BRIGHT CLUTCH.**

what to wear with
BOOT-CUT JEANS*

A **RUGBY-STRIPE SCARF** is a sporty touch and gives **A CARDI** a cool update.

An eye-catching detail like **A FLORAL RING** shows your personality.

AN OVERSIZE PATENT-LEATHER TOTE is classy *and* practical.

PERFECT WHITE SNEAKERS keep the outfit looking neat.

what to wear with
A QUILTED PURSE*

A CROPPED TRENCH looks totally modern over a swingy skirt.

Since your bag is the ultimate classic, buck tradition with **FLASHY AVIATORS.**

A WATCH with a large face plays off the boyfriend trend.

BRIGHT ESPADRILLES add a summery vibe.

WHAT TO WEAR WITH
AN A-LINE SKIRT*

A SWEATSHIRT in a bright color feels more fashion-y.

Pull out your favorite **WINTER HAT** to give your look some playfulness.

A PEARL NECKLACE is cooler when darker beads intertwine with white ones.

*

OXFORD FLATS are a cool contrast to a flouncy mini.

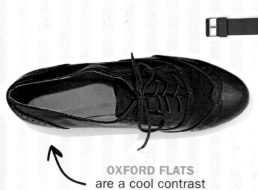

A BOLD RED WATCH gives an extra flash of color every time you move your arm!

WHAT TO WEAR WITH
MARY-JANE HEELS*

Make **A PLAID COAT** more interesting—wear it over **A GRAPHIC TEE** and let a long scarf peek out.

Layering **COLORED BRACELETS** in different sizes creates subtle drama.

A WHITE HOBO BAG is a refined complement to the casual look.

*

CLASSIC GIRL
DAISY

AGE
18

HOMETOWN
New York, NY

STAR SIGN
Aquarius

HOBBIES
Running, writing,
hanging out with friends,
reading fashion blogs

FAVE COLOR
Hunter green

"I stick to traditional, **CLASSIC** silhouettes, but I reinterpret them with **BRIGHT, MODERN ACCESSORIES**."

MY STYLE SOUL MATE

"Blair Waldorf on *Gossip Girl* always looks really polished. She knows how to make every outfit her own by adding pops of color with bright headbands and tights."

SEVENTEEN,
AUGUST 1957

SEVENTEEN,
DECEMBER 1956

MY STYLING SECRET

"Going to boarding school has definitely influenced my look, even outside of class. I stock up on preppy essentials like piped blazers, plaid skirts, and knee-high socks."

my inspirations

MY FAVORITE DECADE

"I love the way girls dressed in the 1950s. The shapes were classic—like V-neck sweaters and pleated or flouncy skirts—but they were also always feminine."

MY MOVIE ICON

"Audrey Hepburn wore nothing but black dresses in *Breakfast at Tiffany's,* but she always looked fantastic. She's iconic not because she took fashion risks but because she stuck to what worked."

MY TOP TREND

"I love the whole equestrian vibe. Riding boots add refined polish to anything from party dresses to jeans and a T-shirt."

MY GO-TO PIECE

"Hunter Wellies instantly pull together any outfit. I wear them with high socks or tights when it's cold and with shorts when it's warm."

85

weekend

"I always want to **look pulled together,** even if I'm just going shopping. A tailored shirt adds polish to casual jeans and boots."

SCHOOL

"A fitted blazer turns a **bright tee** and comfy shorts into something I can wear to class."

DATE

"Nude pumps are super-sophisticated. With a short skirt, they make your **legs look incredibly long.** I plan all my Saturday night date outfits around them."

PARTY

"A rope belt, espadrille wedges, and **a chunky gold necklace** play up the nautical vibe of this dress. It's so fun for any outdoor event."

CLASSIC CELEB-SPIRATION
SELENA GOMEZ

"I like to put a younger twist on the **CLASSIC** chic style." —*Selena*

INSIDER SECRETS TO GETTING SELENA'S STYLE

1
Stick to the basics!
Yes, she likes to experiment with color, but Selena knows that her best colors are the tried-and-true classics: navy, black, and white. They always look crisp and chic.

2
Don't be boring! Selena's look is pared down, but she knows exactly when to mix in some vivid pops of color with a bright scarf or an interesting shoe.

3
Top things off! When other girls only worry about their outfit, Selena also takes care with what she wears over it— a chic trench, cropped leather jacket, or fitted blazer ties her look together.

4
Be "prints" charming! Selena has mastered the art of wearing patterns that don't wear her— an understated plaid or a super-sophisticated pinstripe can add just the right touch of cool.

5
Choose your accessories wisely! This stylish starlet believes that less is more— a pair of hoop earrings and a sparkly cocktail ring are the perfect finish.

seLena's
BEST CLASSIC LOOKS

A tailored red coat adds major drama to a simple outfit.

Sleek dark jeans tucked into tall boots give a casual plaid shirt serious polish.

Play with lengths: A long cami under a cropped jacket paired with awesome stilettos adds dimension.

Subtle accessories and neutral shoes let a vibrant dress take center stage.

Silky shorts, a drapey top, and heels make an unexpected alternative to a party dress.

An animal-print scarf really stands out against a classic white oxford.

A beaded cami and hoops give jeans and boots a bit of bling without going over the top.

Billowy ruffles glam up a sophisticated strapless dress.

classic
STYLING TRICKS TO TRY

Look sophisticated even while testing out new, **FUN WAYS** to mix up your wardrobe.

WEAR YOUR WELLIES!

It doesn't have to rain! Show off your cute rubber boots **BY WEARING THEM WITH LEGGINGS.** It's a sunny look that works in any weather!

ROCK THE PERFECT RED LIPS!

The iconic beauty trick **IS THE CLASSIC WAY TO LOOK SEXY.**

KNOT YOUR TOP!

Reinvent your basic button-down. Unbutton the top two buttons, **THEN KNOT THE BOTTOM.** It's the classic secret to showing a little skin.

CUFF YOUR **SKINNIES!**

Rock a cool French vibe by cuffing the bottom of your skinny pants—
IT'LL HIGHLIGHT LACE-UP FLATS during the day and cute booties at night.

MIX POSH AND SPORTY!

YOUR FAVORITE TEE can be an amazing way to balance a super-luxe piece (like a faux-fur vest).

MAKE SEXY MORE SUBTLE!

Take a low-cut halter dress **INTO CLASSIC TERRITORY** by layering a long-sleeve tee underneath. The dramatic neckline still stands out, but in a more demure way.

YOUR CLASSIC
LOOK BOOK

Polish up your look with inspiration from the runway, the red carpet, *and* the street!

NEW YORK CITY

A capelet makes a super-chic statement—wear it with a tie blouse and plaid pants to take it to the next level!

EMMA ROBERTS

A bubble skirt instantly makes you feel girly—tuck in a slim-fitting shirt to flaunt your curves up top.

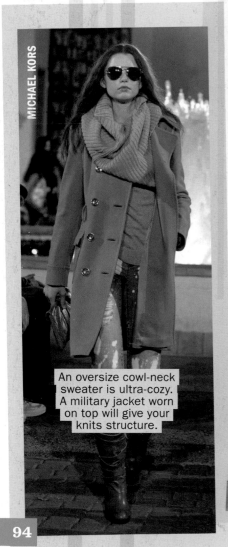

MICHAEL KORS

An oversize cowl-neck sweater is ultra-cozy. A military jacket worn on top will give your knits structure.

MIRANDA COSGROVE

A shrunken tuxedo jacket is the perfect classic pairing for a tee and sparkly mini.

NEW YORK CITY

Shorts are a casual way to show off your legs, but leopard-print shoes give your outfit a "Look at me!" touch.

STELLA MCCARTNEY

Pair a blazer and button-down with a skirt that's slit sky-high! (It's a flirty twist.)

TORY BURCH

Top off breezy summer shorts with a tweedy blazer for major sophistication.

BLAKE LIVELY

A body-conscious black dress is always classic, but a subtle pop of lace makes it extra-sexy.

TOMMY HILFIGER

Tweed from head to toe is the classic girl's uniform.

LAUREN CONRAD

Heels paired with high-waist shorts is retro cool, but a tucked-in blouse polishes the whole look.

LONDON

Trade in your tights for knee socks. A chic scarf wrapped around your neck has a cool Parisian vibe.

VICTORIA JUSTICE

Have fun layering! Wear a white tee over a black tank and top with a trendy blazer cardigan. Don't forget to stack your bracelets too!

RALPH LAUREN

Mega-volume and ruffles bring the drama to a white blouse.

NEW YORK CITY

A solid top worn with vertical stripes on the bottom visually elongates you.

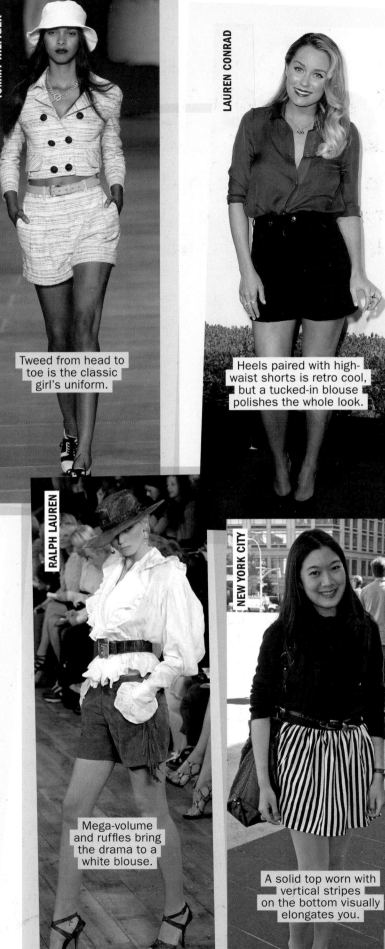

95

SHOP classic

Hit these go-to spots for all your timeless staples!

american eagle outfitters

This store makes jean shopping a breeze by offering denim in almost every shape and wash. You'll be sure to find a fit that makes your body look amazing.

aéropostale

Need to update your wardrobe with some comfy basics? Go here for sporty pieces, like cute tees, tanks, and hoodies.

bass

This classic brand is back! Step up your casual look with saddle oxfords, loafers, and preppy sandals from this trusted footwear brand.

rugby RALPH Lauren

Shop blazers, knits, and rugby shirts (obviously). Plus, you can have your initials embroidered on cardigans, dresses, polo shirts, and more!

GAP

This store has all the essentials, including jeans for every body type—plus you'll find tanks, tees, and sweaters in every color of the rainbow.

abercrombie & fitch

Put a luxe spin on your casual look. This chain's pieces have a preppy feel that's still sexy— check out its super-short minis and super-deep V-necks!

levi's

You'll never get bored browsing the endless denim options here, but it's the classic straight-leg 501s that made them famous (and makes people do a double-take when you wear them).

target

It's the go-to place for the largest selection of bathing suits for your body. Bonus: Its designer clothing lines let you score big-name labels for a lot less.

CHAPTER
five
glam

glam
MUST-HAVES

that let you dazzle 24/7.

The **glam** girl dresses for the spotlight—even if she's just **strutting** the hallways. Turn your everyday look into something dramatic with drop-dead details: sequins that **sparkle,** animal prints that look **luxe,** and heels that go sky high. Don't be afraid to turn a few heads—this is your moment to **shine.**

☑ **SPARKLY DRESS**

When you want to get noticed, glittery dresses always look **RED-CARPET READY.**

☑ DARK SKINNIES

THE MOST VERSATILE PIECE in your closet—they can be super-dressy or flirty-casual.

☑ LEOPARD-PRINT TOP

A kick of animal print **STEPS UP ANY LOOK**—but all you need is one hit!

☑ PLATFORM HEELS

This shape is **FASHION-Y AND CHIC,** yet totally comfortable to walk in.

☑ PENCIL SKIRT

This **CURVE-LOVING STAPLE** makes even a simple tee seem ultra-sexy.

☑ FUR VEST

SPICE UP your everyday look by layering a bit of (faux) fur over it.

☑ ROMPER

It's worth the fashion risk—it makes a **MAJOR STATEMENT** with minor effort!

☑ HIGH-HEEL BOOTS

Whether you wear them with a skirt or over jeans, these boots make your legs look like they **GO ON FOREVER.**

With the right mix of flirty and fun, your **MUST-HAVES** take center stage.

what to wear with
A SPARKLY DRESS*

Don't attempt to tone down a glittering dress. Enhance it instead with some **BOLD JEWELRY.**

PEEP-TOE BOOTIES are a more rebellious version of classic pumps.

Inject some color into your look with a **BRIGHTLY COLORED BAG.**

what to wear with
DARK SKINNIES*

DANGLING EARRINGS make your neck look long and graceful.

A **ONE-SHOULDER DRESSY TOP** shows some skin in a classy way.

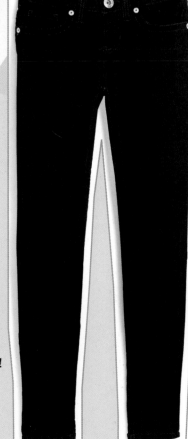

A DETAILED STRAP makes a basic bag more special.

Try **PUMPS** in a glam animal print!

what to wear with
A LEOPARD-PRINT TOP*

A necklace competes too much with a triangle halter top. Instead draw attention with **CHANDELIER EARRINGS.**

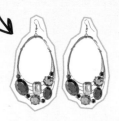

DARK PANTS with embellishments like rhinestones, zippers, and ruching make a cool statement.

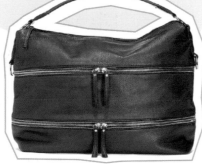

A BAG with multiple zippers is the right amount of rock.

RED HEELS are super-hot and add a feisty splash of color.

what to wear with
PLATFORM HEELS*

A LEATHER JACKET gives **A SLOUCHY SWEATER** some shape.

A PLAYFUL CLUTCH is a surefire way to get people talking!

A SPARKLY MINI is ultra-flirty and shows off your bold heels.

what to wear with A PENCIL SKIRT*

A LAYERED CHAIN NECKLACE gives a ladylike outfit some attitude.

Offset the fanciness of the skirt with **A SUPER-CASUAL SWEATSHIRT**—one with a beaded neckline is a little more special.

A CHUNKY BRACELET makes a bold statement.

A SLOUCHY CLUTCH becomes more engaging when it's made of faux-crocodile skin.

Something **CAGEY AND SEXY** gives a longer skirt more attitude.

what to wear with A FUR VEST*

SUNGLASSES in an unexpected color are especially glamorous.

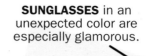

Stay warm without wearing a bulky coat—layer **A SOFT SWEATER** under your fur vest.

Every glam girl needs **A BRIGHT RED BAG.** It's a go-to staple for taking a chic look to the next level.

GRAPHIC PEEP-TOES feel fashion-y in a pretty way. (They're sexy, but not *too* much.)

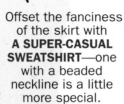

what to wear with
A ROMPER*

A solid romper can feel a little plain—**STATEMENT-MAKING JEWELRY** adds some punch.

A SIMPLE BAG with clean lines is a classic accompaniment to a trendy outfit.

FLAT SANDALS are pretty, but not so showy that they take away from the rest of the outfit.

what to wear with
HIGH-HEEL BOOTS*

Go mod glam with **ART DECO–INSPIRED** jewelry.

A **BRIGHT BAG** in a sleek shape adds oomph without complicating things.

A **SOPHISTICATED JACKET** pairs nicely with more-daring **SNAKESKIN-PRINT PANTS.**

When tucked into knee-high boots, **OVER-THE-TOP LEGGINGS** won't overwhelm your look!

glam girl
REMY

AGE
19

HOMETOWN
New York, NY

STAR SIGN
Cancer

HOBBIES
Fashion blogging, acting,
shopping, working out,
dancing, volunteering

FAVE COLOR
Navy blue

"Being **glam** is really about
being confident.
**IT'S OKAY TO BE
A LITTLE SHOWY**
if you feel good about it."

MY DESIGNER CRUSHES

"Tara Jarmon, Chloé, and Celine—European fashions are so forward-thinking, but the clothes are really beautiful and elegant too."

TARA JARMON

CHLOÉ

CELINE

MY STYLE ICON

"When Anne Hathaway had her big style evolution in *The Devil Wears Prada,* I almost fainted! That movie opened my eyes to new designers and new ways of dressing."

MY FAVORITE FASHION CITY

"I'm lucky to live in New York City, the fashion capital of the world. Walking down the street and seeing what everyone is wearing is like a runway show every day!"

my inspirations

MY STYLE SOUL MATE

"Victoria Beckham is always dressed to the nines. I love that her idea of casual is like most people's glam, and I admire how she's always willing to take a fashion risk."

MY GO-TO PIECE

"All of my money goes toward buying heels. The higher, the better! Christian Louboutin makes the most gorgeous pairs, but I also have favorites from Steve Madden and Forever 21!"

MY BEAUTY OBSESSION

"A coat of lipstick makes you feel glam no matter what you're wearing. Guerlain 03 is the perfect rosy shade. It goes on like a gloss but dries like a lipstick and lasts all night long."

my favorite looks

date

"Guys don't usually understand fashion, so I tend to dress for me, not for him! **A daring scoop-back top** and a fitted skirt with a sexy ruffle make me feel bold and confident."

party

"I love clothes that scream 'Look at me!'—especially when I'm going out. The **hot print and ruffled shoulder** on this dress really bring the drama."

school

"School is like one giant fashion show for me! I pair an unexpected **oversize skull sweater** with cute cargo leggings to get military with an edge. "

weekend

"Just because it's the weekend doesn't mean I have to dress down. I look for **sexy details** like zippers and stitching so I feel comfy but still look chic."

glam celeb-spiration
RIHANNA

"The **thrill** in fashion for me is taking a risk and daring myself to make it work." —*Rihanna*

insider secrets to getting
RIHANNA'S STYLE

one

Try on new shapes! Rihanna is never afraid to play around with all kinds of cool silhouettes, like a strong-shouldered jacket or sexy-tight leggings.

two

Glam up *everything!* Riri adds at least one dressy piece to every outfit, so even a T-shirt looks sleek and on trend.

three

Pile on the bling! Whether it's an oversize necklace or major earrings, her flashy statement jewelry is always a great conversation starter.

four

Sometimes beauty can be your best accessory! Rihanna knows that an over-the-top hairstyle, an electric-red lip, or a super-dramatic smoky eye can make a fashion-y outfit have even more impact.

five

Take your style to new heights! Don't expect to see Rihanna in flats—she wears sky-high stilettos with everything from jeans to minis. They make her entire body look long and lean.

rihanna's
BEST GLAM LOOKS

A bold miniskirt and platform boots are ultra-glam with a shiny metallic top!

Play up a plunging neckline with an oversize pendant and super-long chains.

A simple sweatshirt gets a sexy spin tucked into skinny camo pants.

Offset the sharp angles of a bold, dark blazer with a soft, frothy skirt.

Sleek high-waisted pants and a cropped top are mega-dramatic in a bright-colored palette.

Tons of necklaces and designer shades add a fancy edge to a fitted pencil skirt.

A black statement tee makes a flouncy skirt and cute anklets more fun.

Tie on an animal-print scarf to add a dose of glamour to any outfit.

glam
STYLING TRICKS TO TRY

Strut your stuff with some fashion-forward tips—
they'll instantly STEP UP YOUR LOOK.

WEAR SPARKLE
AT SCHOOL!

Your everyday low-key look will
turn high fashion when you
**MIX A GLITTERY PIECE IN WITH
YOUR CASUAL BASICS.** The secret:
Wear only one main sparkle piece and
offset it with something really casual.

GO BIG
OR GO HOME!

The bigger, the better! **VOLUMINOUS
SHOULDERS DRAW THE EYE UP**
and make your waist look extra tiny.

NAIL
YOUR LOOK!

**A GRAPHIC DESIGN ON YOUR NAILS
GIVES AN UNEXPECTED BURST
OF LUXE** that will get tons of attention.
(It's like a chic accessory!)

FLIRT WITH **FUR!**

NOTHING FEELS MORE GLAM-CHIC THAN SOMETHING FUR (faux, of course!). Toss it over your basics, like jeans and a tee or a simple dress, to create that uptown-posh vibe.

SLIP INTO SHINY SHORTS!

PAIR A SPARKLY PAIR OF SHORTS WITH A PRETTY TOP for an unexpected glam touch.

BUST OUT THE BUSTIER!

A formfitting bustier can go out during the day! **WEAR IT OVER A LONG-SLEEVED SHIRT** for a covered-up look that feels super-dramatic.

your glam
LOOK BOOK

Steal these tricks from the runway, the red carpet, *and* the street—these looks are sure to cause a stir!

CHRISTIAN DIOR

A bright halter dress draws attention to your shoulders, while ankle-tie sandals add an extra flash of color.

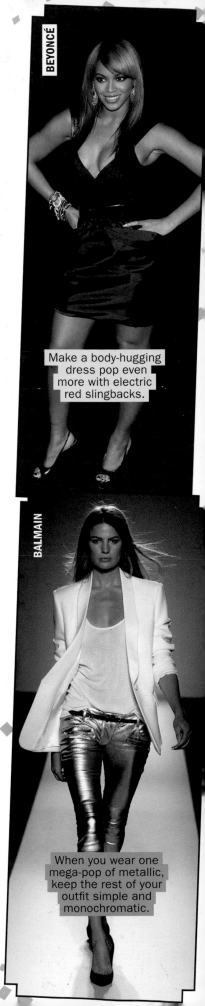

BEYONCÉ

Make a body-hugging dress pop even more with electric red slingbacks.

DOLCE & GABBANA

Leopard print and sparkle are high impact, but the swinging skirt and dangly earrings are totally sweet.

ALY MICHALKA

One-shoulder dresses are glam and fierce. Throw in curve-clinging pleats and you'll turn heads all night.

BADGLEY MISCHKA

Silky shorts in a muted color have an understated elegance.

BALMAIN

When you wear one mega-pop of metallic, keep the rest of your outfit simple and monochromatic.

WILLIAM RAST

A major dose of fur—like a dramatic scarf—takes a windbreaker and mini to a glam level.

KIM KARDASHIAN

A tailored blazer over a printed dress feels sleek. The boots give this look an approachable vibe.

NEW YORK CITY

Shiny shorts in a quirky print are playful. Mix them with simple, solid items already in your closet so your look doesn't feel costumey.

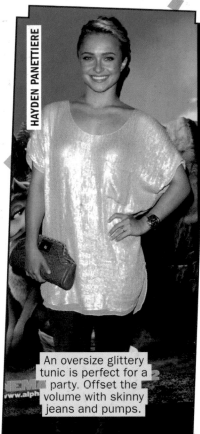

HAYDEN PANETTIERE

An oversize glittery tunic is perfect for a party. Offset the volume with skinny jeans and pumps.

EMMA STONE

A sequined minidress makes you the hottest girl in the room. Long sleeves balance the super-short hem, and nude heels stretch your legs.

VERSACE

Experiment with a cutout top—it won't seem like *too* much when worn with a simple below-the-knee skirt.

NEW YORK CITY

When you throw on a leopard coat, even rain boots can look completely glam!

GUCCI

Spice up a little black dress with gold accents. The finishing touch? Bold red lipstick.

117

SHOP glam

Hit these go-to spots for all your eye-catching pieces!

zara

asos

macy's

forever 21

This European chain is inspired by designer trends and is the first to bring the hottest looks to the racks. Check out its huge selection of runway-inspired blazers and jackets!

Finally! The British Web site asos.com is now available in America! It's creating a ton of buzz for chic designs that you won't find anywhere else.

Check out the Material Girl line, designed by Madonna and her daughter Lourdes, for sparkly cardigans and faux fur! Plus, you'll find a ton of evening dress options for homecoming and prom!

You'll have a tough time finding a sweeter deal anywhere else! Check out this store's embellished tops, flirty minis, and blingy accessories!

bcbg

Young Hollywood is obsessed with BCBG. Got a splurge-worthy event coming up, like a Sweet Sixteen, prom, or graduation party? Find a dress here that'll make you stand out in the crowd.

guess

Going to the movies with your guy or grabbing dinner with a group? This store is known for its sexy jeans and tanks, so you'll look hot but not too done up.

aldo

Take your whole outfit to a higher level (literally) with this shoe line's playful super-high pumps and sexy platform boots.

claire's

When you need a funky bracelet or a statement necklace, this one-stop jewelry shop has everything you'll ever need to accessorize at awesome prices.

CHAPTER
S1X
indie

Indie girls take pride in being a little **unexpected** and putting things together in **surprising** ways. So have **fun** playing with proportions, **reinventing** the finds from your local thrift store, and DIY-ing some **cool** pieces. Because you know that when you push the envelope, you pull out your best looks!

indie
MUST-HAVES
EIGHT ESSENTIAL PIECES
that leave your closet overflowing with personality.

☑ **HIGH-WAISTED JEANS**

They have a **BUILT-IN, LAID-BACK FEEL** that's fashion-y but not obnoxious.

DRAPEY CARDIGAN

Relaxed yet polished—the perfect piece to **THROW OVER PRETTY MUCH ANYTHING.**

OXFORD SHOES

These shoes are **PART RETRO, PART BOYISH**— and look super-cute with cuffed jeans.

PLAID SHIRT

Soften its masculine feel by choosing a **SLIM-FITTING STYLE** that shows off your curves.

SHORTS

High-waisted shorts are **AN INTERESTING ALTERNATIVE** to a skirt.

CREWNECK SWEATSHIRT

When everything else in your wardrobe is of-the-moment, buck the trend with **THIS CLASSIC STAPLE.**

WEDGE BOOTS

Wedges are the perfect way to add **COOLNESS (AND HEIGHT!)** to any look.

RETRO DRESS

Go for a dress that has tons of charm— one that's **FLOUNCY AND FEMININE.**

Add these pieces to your MUST-HAVES for styles with no boundaries.

what to wear with HIGH-WAISTED JEANS*

HEART-SHAPED EARRINGS offer the cutest little touch of personality.

Psst! You don't need a glasses prescription to rock these **COOL FRAMES.**

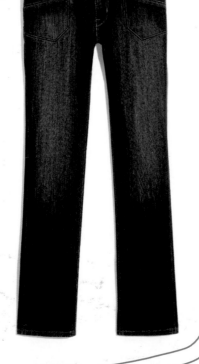

A BOLD-STRIPE SWEATER that hits at the hips looks chic and shows off the jean's high rise.

FRINGE SLINGBACKS add some fun texture.

what to wear with A DRAPEY CARDIGAN*

DIFFERENT-LENGTH TOPS look more pulled together when they're all cinched with a chic skinny belt.

A CHAIN-STRAP LEATHER BAG adds a tiny bit of polish.

ZIPPERED LEGGINGS are a cool step up from a basic pair.

BLACK-AND-WHITE SPECTATORS have uptown-meets-downtown flair.

what to wear with
A CREWNECK SWEATSHIRT*

A BRIGHT SCARF adds interest to an open neckline.

ANTIQUE-Y VINTAGE PINS are an easy way to put your own stamp on anything!

Do the casual thing without looking sloppy. **SHORT SHORTS** with a tapered bottom look great and flash major leg.

Create your own DIY project—use bottles of paint to make **SPLATTER FLATS.** They're inexpensive and one of a kind.

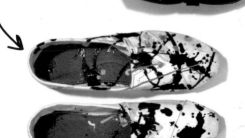

what to wear with
OXFORD SHOES*

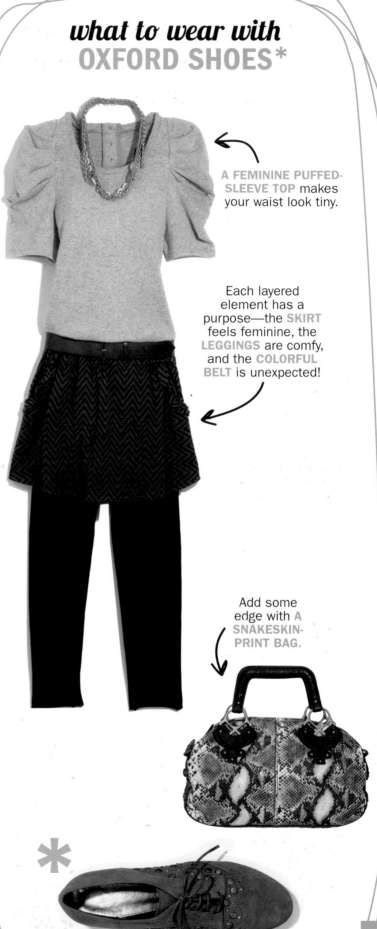

A FEMININE PUFFED-SLEEVE TOP makes your waist look tiny.

Each layered element has a purpose—the **SKIRT** feels feminine, the **LEGGINGS** are comfy, and the **COLORFUL BELT** is unexpected!

Add some edge with **A SNAKESKIN-PRINT BAG.**

what to wear with
SHORTS*

BUTTERFLY SLEEVES are dramatic and add a little volume up top.

*

Scour vintage shops and thrift stores for **UNIQUE ACCESSORIES** that no one else will have.

Wear **FLAT BOOTIES** with tights to show off your legs without showing too much.

what to wear with
WEDGE BOOTS*

These **CHAIN EARRINGS** are a funky counterpoint to such a fancy top.

An eye-catching trim is just the thing to step up a **DRAPEY CAMI.** (A long compass necklace is a distinctive touch.)

Rough up this feminine look a little more with **SLOUCHY JEANS** and a **CHUNKY WATCH.**

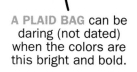

*

A PLAID BAG can be daring (not dated) when the colors are this bright and bold.

what to wear with
A PLAID SHIRT*

JEWELED BANGLES add a pop of glam!

Mix and match patterns—this **FLORAL** works with plaid when the two share similar colors.

A SOLID, OVERSIZE BAG grounds the entire look.

QUIRKY HEELS give any outfit a more personal feel.

what to wear with
A RETRO DRESS*

EMBELLISHED GOLD HOOPS frame your face in a pretty way.

Play with prints by layering **A STRIPED CARDIGAN** on top.

The zippers and dramatic shape make this **HANDBAG** retro-cool.

STACKED WOODEN HEELS are chic *and* earthy.

indie girl
STEPHANIE

AGE
22

HOMETOWN
New York, NY

STAR SIGN
Gemini

HOBBIES
Writing, taking pictures, reading, sketching, skateboarding

FAVE COLOR
Black

" I'm way more **INFLUENCED BY EMOTIONS, ART, AND THE PEOPLE** *around me* than by trends. "

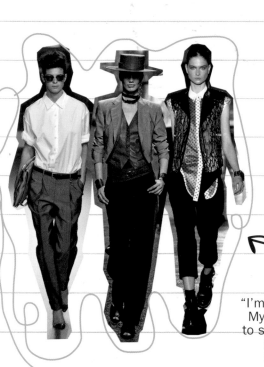

MY FAVORITE DECADE
"The '90s were all about chipped nail polish, grungy hair, and cool bands like the Cranberries. Some days when I get dressed, I totally embrace that feeling of teen angst!"

MY STYLING SECRET
"I'm totally down with the androgyny thing. My boyfriend is a musician, and we love to swap clothes. I steal his long sweaters and ripped denim, and he borrows my sequined stuff for performing."

my inspirations

MY FASHION OBSESSION
"I wear Converse almost every day. It amazes me how they're completely classic and full of nostalgia but still so modern at the same time."

MY SECRET WEAPON
"It feels magical when I find the perfect vintage piece, like my chunky knit sweater coat. It has a history and makes my look unique."

MY STYLE SOUL MATES
"Patti Smith and Debbie Harry are such iconic rock-and-roll chicks. I always try to channel them and think about how they'd style themselves when I'm getting dressed."

MY FASHION PHILOSOPHY
"My outfits can't be too serious. I'm a big fan of nonsense and silliness—like *Alice in Wonderland*. I love to have fun, even if it's sometimes a little impractical, like with a glittery headpiece or big puffy sweater."

my favorite looks

party

"Everyone does the little black dress for a party. I'd rather show up in something unconventional, **like a little white dress.** Dark tights and funky heels up the cool factor even more."

date

"I'd never wear what's expected on a date. This **vintage jacket** adds an air of romance, but the shorts and tee keep it casual and cool."

weekend

"I'm intrigued by an eclectic mix of graphics and textures. The **printed shorts** are totally fun, and the flannel is cozy to wear chilling out in the park."

school

"I love **sequins for daytime**—they make me feel excited to get dressed! And they look awesome paired with utilitarian things, like this versatile army jacket."

indie celeb-spiration

EMMA WATSON

"I like to make a statement and *experiment*, because fashion should be all about fun." —*Emma*

insider secrets to getting
EMMA'S STYLE

1

Dress your age! Some celebs look like they're trying to be more grown-up than they are. But not Emma! She embraces her youthfulness with playful dresses and fun bags!

2

Flatter your figure! Emma focuses on trends that work for her, not just what's hot on the runways. To dress her small frame, she picks simple silhouettes and small details that don't overwhelm her.

3

Edit your outfits! Emma knows that everything she wears says something about her style, so you'll never see her wearing careless piles of jewelry or shoes that are a little off. She's pared down to perfection.

4

Pick one amazing piece! Emma's essential fashion trick is to build her look around something specific— an incredible dress or a dramatic bag. She never wears things that compete for attention.

5

Look for quirky details! Emma opts for things that seem just slightly unusual, like asymmetrical hemlines or creative prints. They take her outfits to the next level.

BEST INDIE LOOKS

Put a funky twist on traditional pieces by mixing textures, like classic twill and edgy leather.

Dramatic jewelry thrown over a rich fabric like velvet gives off a glam-meets-rock vibe.

Stand out without showing a ton of skin. Play with subtle midriff cutouts and put a racy spin on black pumps.

Keep jewelry and makeup minimal with an ultra-flashy frock. You're already shining!

When a dress is simple, enhance it with a strong accessory that reflects your playful personality.

Wear slim pants under a girly dress to reinvent it in an indie way. (A misbuttoned cardi keeps the dress from looking too sweet!)

Make a super-short hemline more demure by adding solid tights underneath.

Take a cue from London street style by using a blazer, fedora, and tights to chic up a pretty skirt.

indie STYLING TRICKS TO TRY

STEP UP YOUR OWN UNIQUE STYLE with these cool tricks.

TRY BRIGHT LEGWEAR!

Freshen up a dark skirt by wearing tights in an electric hue. **IT WILL EXAGGERATE YOUR STYLE** and show off your legs!

DRAW ON EVERYTHING!

Let your personality spill all over your favorite clothes. **DOODLING ON WHITE SNEAKERS OR DENIM SHORTS** gives your clothes special meaning.

TIE ON A SCARF!

A scarf is an understated way to pull an entire look together. When you **GO WITH ONE THAT HAS A FUN PATTERN,** it punctuates your outfit in a surprising way!

MIX UP YOUR PATTERNS!

Flash your cute and quirky side by having fun with prints. **EDGY ZEBRA CAN TOTALLY WORK WITH GLAM METALLICS**—together they create a combo that feels more exciting than either would alone.

PLAY WITH PROPORTIONS!

TOP A SLIM-FITTING ITEM WITH A LOOSE ONE. The body-hugging silhouette underneath ensures you won't get lost in all that volume.

WEAR SOCKS WITH SANDALS!

Breathe new life into your summer heels by wearing them with socks. **THEY KEEP TOES WARM AND ADD A LITTLE TEXTURE!**

your indie LOOK BOOK

Even creative girls like you could use a muse. Let these looks from the red carpet, the runway, *and* the street be your launching pad.

HAYLEY WILLIAMS

Oversize bows are youthful, but scattered all over, they punch up your feminine look.

VANCOUVER, CANADA

Mix your styles! A classic trench, preppy skirt, bold tights, and glam hair accessory can totally work together.

TWENTY8TWELVE

A flirty vintage-print dress gets a little edge when paired with a black lace shrug.

WHITNEY PORT

Throw on a shimmery blazer to polish up your favorite jeans—cuffing them will highlight your cute shoes!

RODARTE

Feeling extra-daring? Then play around with patterns and lengths to set yourself apart from the crowd.

NEW YORK CITY

Eye-catching prints can draw attention to your best features—like a tiny waist.

High-waist shorts are super-dramatic. Tuck in your top and cinch with a cute belt to flaunt this fashiony silhouette.

A top with voluminous shoulders feels very Victorian. Balance it with a slim-fitting skirt.

Leather shorts have a tough vibe. Give your naughty look a nice touch with a textured sweater.

Neutral stripes come to life with a red blouse (and a little pin adds even more life!).

Put a fashion-forward twist on the jumpsuit trend by going head to toe in bold stripes.

A quirky colorblock dress packs an even bigger punch when it's not over-accessorized: Black booties and a slouchy knit hat are just enough.

Preppy argyle and sweet floral create a style that's filled with personality.

Take a button-down up a few notches—red shoes and a fedora will get you there!

139

SHOP *indie*

Hit these go-to spots for all your fun staples!

etsy

Infuse your look with fashion creativity! On etsy.com, you can buy one-of-a-kind pieces from independent designers.

modcloth

Visit modcloth.com for retro dresses that have a sweet yet quirky vibe. It's perfect for finding a party dress that flaunts your individual taste.

urban outfitters

As if a cool assortment of vintage-inspired clothing wasn't reason enough to shop here, this store has an amazing shoe collection—a fun mix of funky heels, unique boots, and delicate flats.

LF stores

If you thrive on pushing the fashion envelope, this is the perfect place to find a crazy mix of styles. Shop here for dresses that none of your friends will already have.

madewell

With Alexa Chung as a guest designer, this store is your go-to spot for an eclectic mix of clothes that work the hipster-chic look. The brand is known for making pieces with unique vintage details.

converse

Make a sweet dress more casual or add a retro punch to jeans. The classic white-capped sneaker has been reinvented with cool patterns and bright colors, and the company even collaborated on designs with musicians.

buffalo exchange

You'll find plenty of hidden treasures at amazing prices at this hip thrift-store chain. Not only will you look good, you'll feel good knowing that the store recycles its clothing.

american apparel

Neon leggings? Done. Patterned over-the-knee socks? Check. Striped tee? Got that. This store is filled with all your staple pieces in a huge assortment of colors, unique prints, and different fabrics.

U
ACC

YOUR ULTIMATE ESSORY GUIDE

MUST-HAVE
SHOES

The perfect shoes give you the confidence to put your best foot forward. Here are the shapes that'll step up *your* look!

☑ **OXFORDS**

The boy-meets-girl look is super-hot—and this new shape will add a trendy twist to any outfit.

☑ **FLATS**

They can be girly, classic, or even wild—but above all else, they're the cute way to be comfy!

☑ **SNEAKERS**

Sporty can totally be chic—just choose kicks in cool patterns and colors for maximum style impact.

☑ **HEELS**

Not only are they super-sexy, but they make your legs look miles long!

☑ **WEDGES**

They give any look a modern feel—thankfully, they're easy to walk in!

☑ BOAT SHOES

Originally these were the true preppy standard—but the new versions of this classic can be completely edgy or boho!

☑ SANDALS

Swap flip-flops for flat, strappy sandals to take your laid-back look up a notch.

☑ MOTO BOOTS

Your go-to when you want to kick up your style. They look as good with jeans as they do with a miniskirt.

☑ HIGH-TOPS

Tuck skinny jeans into these stand-out sneakers when you want to let your fun style pop!

DO...

✓ **Pick the right shoes to flatter your figure!** Heels lift and shape your booty, and nude shades make your legs look longer!

✓ **Use shoes to add color!** It's tempting to stick with versatile black and brown, but red or blue can be just as universal (and a lot more fun!).

DON'T...

✗ **Try on only one shoe of a pair!** It's true that one foot is usually bigger than the other!

✗ **Sacrifice comfort for fashion!** If you can't walk in those super-high heels, you'll never wear them—so what's the point?!?

MUST-HAVE
BAGS

**Carry your stuff in style!
The right bag can add a mega-dose
of personality to your outfit.**

☑ **HOBO**

The perfect mix of
slouchy and pretty!
It's roomy enough
to fit your stuff, but
small enough not to
overwhelm your look!

☑ **SHOULDER**

Tucked under your
arm, it always looks
feminine and chic.

☑ **CLUTCH**

Not just for a night out—
don't be afraid to take
this cute piece to a pizza
date or pop it in your
everyday tote!

☑ **CROSS-BODY**

This modern
purse looks best
when it hits right
at your hip!

☑ BACKPACK

A backpack doesn't need to be *just* utilitarian—look for bright ones to give your school look some oomph.

☑ SHORT-HANDLED

When you need to dress to impress, pull out this bag—it's sophisticated and polished.

☑ TOTE

During the school year, it's perfect for carrying your books; in the summer, it can hold all your beach essentials!

☑ MESSENGER

The extra compartments keep you organized—but the relaxed shape makes you look effortlessly cool.

DO...

✓ **Add your own touch!** Tie a pretty scarf on the handle or pin on some fun buttons all over.

✓ **Invest in one really good bag.** If you pick one in a neutral color and a classic shape, it'll last you forever!

DON'T...

✗ **Play it safe!** An inexpensive bag is a risk-free way to try out a bright color or a crazy trend!

✗ **Buy a bag that's not functional.** If you know you like to carry everything with you, make sure you have room for it—nothing looks worse than a bag that's busting at the seams!

MUST-HAVE
JEWELRY

Decorate yourself! Fashion smarties know how to pick the perfect baubles to create a look that's all their own.

 **RINGS**

Raid your mom's jewelry box for unique pieces that none of your friends will have.

Want to make a statement? Talk with your hands by slipping on an oversize cocktail ring!

Skinny rings are made for stacking! Slide on a bunch for a pretty, artsy effect.

 **BRACELETS**

Whether it's thin bangles or friendship bracelets, pile them on! Two (or eight!) is always better than one!

Charm bracelets let you express what you love!

Bangles that are big and bold can anchor an entire look! (Sometimes they're the only accessory you need.)

✓ NECKLACES

Pretty, colorful beads can perk up any neutral outfit and give your look a global feel!

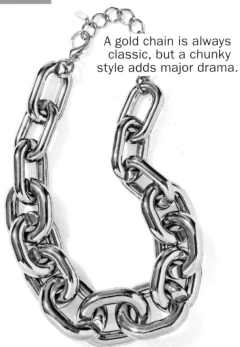

A gold chain is always classic, but a chunky style adds major drama.

A delicate pendant is a sweet, personal finishing touch.

Hoops draw attention to your face. Pick a pair in a bold color—they'll pop!

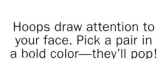

✓ EARRINGS

Bright studs add a subtle touch of color without competing with other jewelry.

A long pair of chandelier earrings always gets attention— they catch the light every time you move your head!

DO...

✓ **Mix vintage pieces** with newer styles to get a one-of-a-kind look.

✓ **Try a trend!** Adding a few ultra-trendy pieces or inexpensive jewelry to your look is a fun way to update your whole style.

DON'T...

✗ **Pile on too much!** Adding a billion pieces actually takes away from your look—people don't know what to focus on!

✗ **Be afraid to use jewelry in surprising ways:** A stud earring can become a cute pin, and a long beaded necklace can turn into a chic bracelet!

MUST-HAVE
HATS

The secret to turning heads is easy!
Just top off your look with one of
these cute styles.

☑ CAP

Feeling sporty? Guys can't
resist a girl in a baseball cap—
so fun with your ponytail
sticking out the back!

☑ BUCKET

Make any casual look a little
more preppy with a colorful
fisherman-style hat!

☑ BEANIE

This colorful knit
piece is surprisingly
rocker—wear it
with a leather jacket
or cozy flannel.

☑ BOMBER

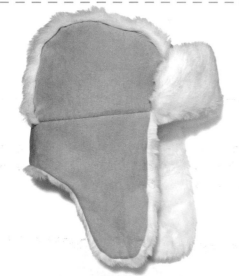

This snuggly style looks
adorable and keeps
your ears toasty-warm!

☑ MILITARY

A fashion risk worth taking!
It turns a tee and jeans into
something unexpected.

☑ NEWSBOY

Straight-on, it has a classic feel; turned slightly to the side, it suddenly becomes more playful!

☑ FEDORA

A fashion girl's essential: Clip a feather or floral pin to the band to make it your own.

☑ BERET

Add some *ooh-la-la* to your style with this French must-have.

☑ KNIT

The slouchy shape feels totally romantic—soft, breezy, and chill (just the way you want to be on the weekend).

DO...

✓ **Hide a bad hair day** by throwing on a playful hat! (No one has to know. . . .)

✓ **Steal from your brother's or BF's closet!** Who looks cuter than you in his boyish beanie? No one!

DON'T...

✗ **Wear a hat that overwhelms you.** Pick a style, height, and brim size that's proportionate to your head.

✗ **Top off an already busy outfit.** A hat is a major style commitment—you have to respect its place at the center of your outfit!

MUST-HAVE
SUNGLASSES

Hello, Hollywood! Who knew such a small accessory could add such mega glam?

 **OVERSIZE**

This celebrity staple screams, "Look at me—I'm major!"

 **AVIATOR**

This classic shape never goes out of style.

 **SQUARE**

They have that retro-cool feel and give your summer outfit an instant shot of chic.

ROUND

This old-school look offers a dose of vintage quirkiness.

CAT'S EYE

Part vintage, part modern—completely cool.

WRAPAROUND

The sleek shape makes any look feel more fashion-forward.

NOVELTY

Hearts? Stars? Whatever! Go for an unexpected shape when you just want to have a little fun.

WAYFARER

In black, they have that mysterious, cool-girl vibe— in a punchy color, they suddenly feel super-flirty!

DO...

✓ **Pick a shape that flatters your face!** Rounder shades look great with angular faces, and square shades are perfect for rounder faces.

✓ **Dare to wear shades all year-round!** These aren't just a summer staple—a pair of aviators looks so cool with a warm, wooly scarf!

DON'T...

✗ **Blow your budget!** Keep your eyes on the runway and score designer-inspired styles for a lot less at your favorite bargain stores.

✗ **Stick to one style!** Branch out and pick a few different pairs to suit each of your fashion personalities.

MUST-HAVE
OTHER STUFF

Great style is in the details! These are the add-ons that can make your look so much more exciting.

☑ SOCKS

Cute socks are too good to hide! Layer them over tights or under sandals so they stand out.

☑ TIGHTS

Go for graphic patterns in bright colors to play up your great legs and fun personality!

☑ SCARVES

A warm, knitted scarf will keep you cozy—and a bright color will keep winter blues at bay!

Add texture and sparkle to your look with a scarf in an eye-catching metallic.

A scarf in a pretty print gives your style some pop.

HAIR ACCESSORIES

A headband is a bad hair day's best friend! Slip one on, and you have an instant style!

Switch up your basic barrettes and rubber bands with a flirty bow or a pretty flower instead!

Hair clips with little sparkly jewels give your style sweet personality.

BELTS

A wide shape is perfect for cinching in billowy dresses and tops.

A thin belt is a key finishing touch for your favorite skinny jeans.

DO...

✓ **Feel free to mix things up!** Turn your favorite scarf into a headband or your best hair tie into a bracelet.

✓ **Go for color!** A bright anything (scarf, tights!) will always make a bigger impact than black.

DON'T...

✗ *Overmix!* If brown leather is at the center of your accessory palette, be wary of throwing giant silver sequins into the pot!

✗ **Sink into a rut.** You might feel comfortable wearing a scarf every day, but where's the fashion fun in that?!?

More pieces to suit your style!

girly ACCESSORIES

Look for pretty pastels, flowers, and bows that show off what a fashion sweetheart you are.

boho
ACCESSORIES
Earthy tones and rich fabrics
(like leather) give off
that laid-back/luxe vibe.

CLASSIC
ACCESSORIES
Bright stripes and plaids
energize your polished style
in a totally fresh way!

edgy
ACCESSORIES

When you want to rock out your outfit, slip on eye-catching pieces with a fierce attitude.

glam
ACCESSORIES
Let your style dazzle any crowd—go for high-shine pieces and ultra-bold details.

indie
ACCESSORIES

Pick quirky pieces with
maximum fashion impact—the object
is to leave people talking!

YOUR ULTIMATE T GUIDE

FIND YOUR PERFECT FIT:
JEANS

The right pair can make you feel amazing.
Here's how to get the ones that hug
and highlight all of your favorite features.

CURVY ALL OVER

TALL

Go for **STRAIGHT-LEG JEANS**—their classic fit skims curves without pinching.

STRETCHY DENIM makes you feel slim and sexy—not swallowed up!

Waists that sit **HIGHER ON YOUR HIPS** will make your legs look even longer.

RIPPED DENIM looks laid-back and cute, and it draws attention to your awesome legs!

Make sure your jeans aren't too short—look for **AN INSEAM OF 32" OR LONGER.**

CURVY BUTT

CONTRAST STITCHING looks polished and defines your booty's shape.

Streamline your curves with **DARK-WASH JEANS**

CURVY TUMMY

Jeans that **DIP IN THE MIDDLE** but pull up higher on the sides keep you from getting that jelly roll!

Choose a **WIDE WAISTBAND** for extra comfort—no pinching or digging!

FLAT BUTT

DETAILING ON THE POCKETS will visually fill out your booty.

FADING UNDER YOUR BUTT will make your tush look higher and perkier.

CURVY THIGHS

Go for a **SOLID WASH** with no fading—the dark color trims you all over!

TROUSER JEANS won't cling to your thighs. Plus, the wider legs give you a lean look!

PETITE

LIGHT WASHES draw your eye down to make your legs look longer.

Go for **ANKLE-LENGTH JEANS** to avoid any unflattering bunching.

CURVY HIPS

A MEDIUM RISE that hits above your hip bone eliminates any muffin top.

BOOTCUT JEANS balance and slim your hips.

MORE JEANS FOR YOU!

	CURVY ALL OVER	TALL	CURVY BUTT	CURVY TUMMY
SCHOOL	 Go for cool moto jeans—the seams highlight legs in a slimming way.	 A little distressing gives your legs an athletic look.	 Pockets that sit high on your tush make it look more shapely.	 The high waist covers your tummy, while the low, curvy pockets draw the eye downward.
DATE	 Wear these flare-leg jeans with heels and your legs will look crazy-long and lean!	 Dark skinnies will make your legs look like they go on forever!	 Choose indigo and black rinses— they make your butt look slimmer but still perky!	 Shading and subtle tears draw attention away from the tummy!
WEEKEND	 Go for fitted jeans with a little bit of stretch for extra comfort.	 Distressed boot-cut jeans are low-key and won't overwhelm your frame.	 Jeggings snuggly flaunt your curves, and the stretch won't create bulge above the waistband.	 Super-stretchy jeans— even in a light color—hug your body in the *right* places!

No matter what the occasion, there is a pair of jeans ut there to perfectly flatter every figure.

FLAT BUTT	CURVY THIGHS	PETITE	CURVY HIPS

Light washes and fading under your butt add major curves!

Bell-shaped bottoms balance out your curves.

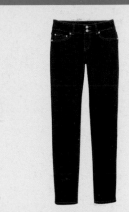

Choose skinny jeans that hug your cute curves rather than cover them up.

Trouser jeans lie flat across your hips, giving your whole figure a streamlined look.

Large pockets positioned far apart sculpt your tush.

Try slim straight jeans— they make you look sleek without cutting you off at the ankles!

Fading down the center visually elongates your legs!

Straight jeans give a leaner fit while still flaunting your shape.

The angled detailing on the pockets makes your booty pop!

Wide-leg jeans give your lower half a super-sleek silhouette.

Cropped jeans look perfectly proportionate on your small frame.

Boot-cut jeans in a dark wash are insanely flattering!

FIND YOUR PERFECT FIT:
SWIMSUITS

When you love the way your body looks in
your bathing suit, you're bound to turn heads!

A HALTER TOP cinches your chest together to add cleavage.

LIGHT PADDING on top makes your bust a focal point without looking unnatural.

WELL-PLACED RUFFLES that cascade down the body give your figure some curves.

PEEKABOO OPENINGS add visual interest and help fill you out.

SMALL BUST

BOYISH

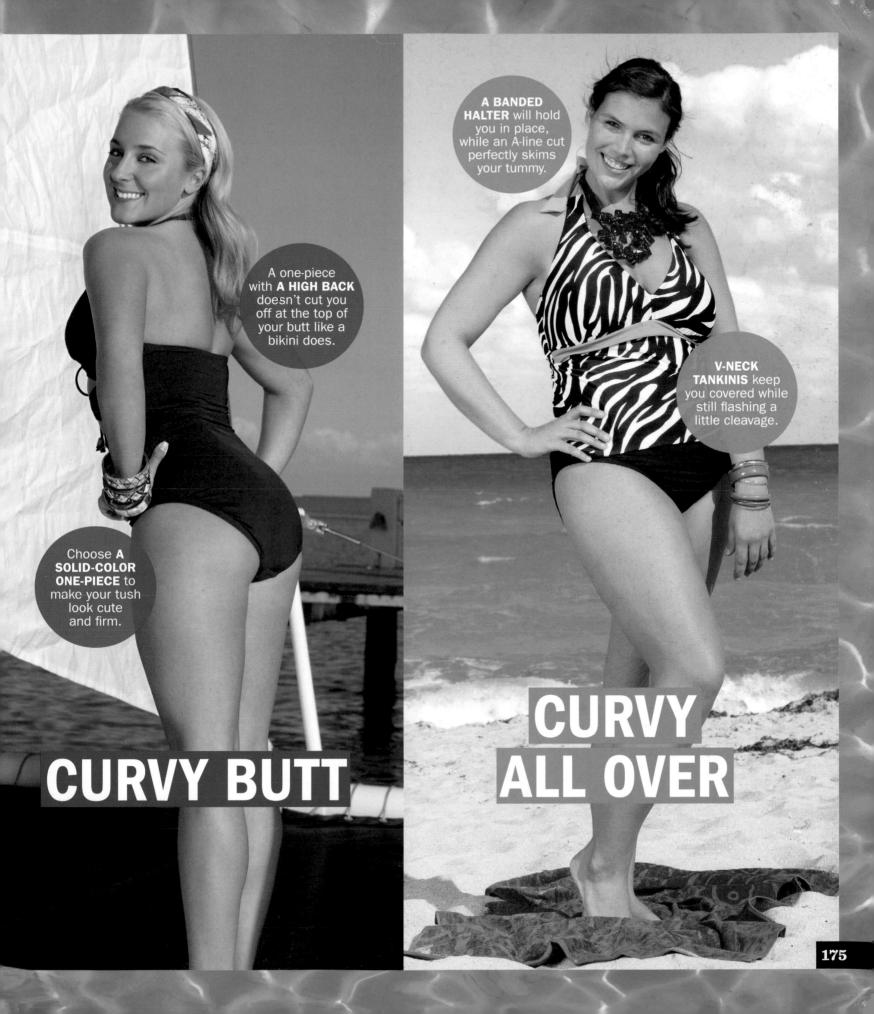

A one-piece with **A HIGH BACK** doesn't cut you off at the top of your butt like a bikini does.

Choose **A SOLID-COLOR ONE-PIECE** to make your tush look cute and firm.

CURVY BUTT

A BANDED HALTER will hold you in place, while an A-line cut perfectly skims your tummy.

V-NECK TANKINIS keep you covered while still flashing a little cleavage.

CURVY ALL OVER

A patterned **BANDEAU TOP** supports you but still shows a flirty peek of cleavage.

A GRAPHIC PATTERN all over makes your top and bottom look proportionate.

FULL BUST

WIDE STRIPES on top draw attention upward and balance out a fuller bottom.

Bottoms with **SIDE TIES** allow you to adjust your fit—so there's no squeezing!

CURVY HIPS

A SMALL PRINT will add definition to your bottom and create the illusion of a fuller shape.

GATHERS at the top of your butt perk up your booty so it looks rounder.

A LOW-CUT NECKLINE draws the eye up to your pretty decolletage.

RUCHING across the tummy cinches in your waist and camouflages curves!

FLAT BUTT

CURVY TUMMY

MORE SWIMSUITS FOR YOU!

	SMALL BUST	**BOYISH**	**CURVY BUTT**	**CURVY ALL OVER**
BIKINI	Allover ruffles on the cups add volume for a rounder look.	A cinched top and ruffles on the bottom create some oomph!	Choose a boy-cut bottom in a dark color for a sleek effect.	Ties at the neck and waist let yo[u] adjust your suit for the perfect fit
TANKINI	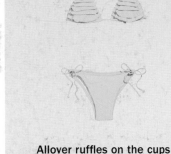Light padding up top makes your bust look fuller.	Bold, oversize prints visually fill out your frame.	Dark, high-cut bottoms slim your roundest area.	A-line cuts give you a leaner look and still show your shape.
ONE-PIECE	Horizontal stripes enhance a smaller bust!	A sexy cutout monokini practically draws curves on your body!	Highlight your waist (and not your butt) with a polka-dot tie.	The pretty folds in front nip in your waist without clinging.

Whether you want to flaunt it all or go for a little more coverage, there's a bathing suit out there for every body type.

FULL BUST	CURVY HIPS	FLAT BUTT	CURVY TUMMY

Wave good-bye to spilling and sagging with an underwire top.

Stretchy tabs on the bottom's sides keep you from getting ugly dents.

A twirly ruffle and busy print fill out your booty.

Drawstrings let you raise the bottoms higher to cover your tummy.

A higher-cut V-neck top minimizes the size of your bust.

A slightly shorter top shows off a sexy peek of tummy.

The plaid print makes your tush seem fuller.

Tiered ruffles are a sweet, girly way to hide your tummy.

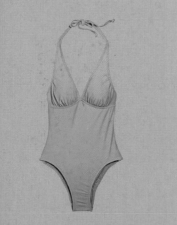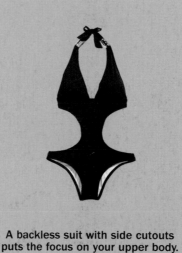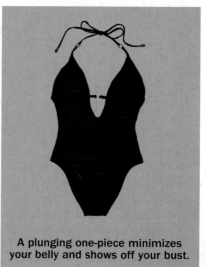

A halter top that ties customizes your cleavage for a comfy fit.

Tie sides let you raise the cut to draw attention up to your waist.

A backless suit with side cutouts puts the focus on your upper body.

A plunging one-piece minimizes your belly and shows off your bust.

FIND YOUR PERFECT FIT:

BRAS AND UNDIES

The key to loving your look starts with what's underneath it all!
Find the perfect bras and undies for *your* body here!

Choose a bra **WITH LIGHT PADDING** that flatters your bust.

A CUP

SOFT-CUP BRALETTES fit snuggly against your breasts so there are no awkward gaps.

GREAT BRAS FOR YOU!

DAY

Plunging cups with padding give you a smidge of cleavage under a low-cut tee.

NIGHT

The lined demi cup gives you a natural-looking boost.

SPORT

Look for a soft fabric with a little stretch to keep you in place.

Look for bras with **A BENDABLE UNDERWIRE** (or none!) to lift you up without digging.

B CUP

WIDE-SET STRAPS give you a lift and won't awkwardly peek out of a scoop-neck top.

DAY

A bra with a little padding on the sides pushes you together to give you some cleavage.

NIGHT

A strapless bra with a lace band holds you up without creating lumps.

SPORT

Look for stretchy side panels for support and a tighter fit.

A bra with a **GOOD UNDERWIRE** will lift your breasts and give them shape.

C CUP

Choose **DOUBLE STRAPS**—the outer one will hold you in while the inner one will pull you up.

GREAT BRAS FOR YOU!

DAY

A V-shaped bra flatters your bust—higher-cut cups prevent you from spilling out.

NIGHT

A full-cup bra can still be sexy—look for a lower cut and a front clasp.

SPORT

A racerback holds you up without putting strain on your shoulders.

D CUP

Look for a bra with only a **LITTLE BIT OF STRETCH**—it'll keep you perky and supported.

A MINIMIZING BRA can make you look a full size smaller.

DAY

Wider straps give full busts a pretty lift without being too pushed up.

NIGHT

Look for multiple hooks in the back to give your strapless a perfect fit.

SPORT

Foam cups hold your breasts in place so they won't bounce.

PERFECT UNDIES FOR *EVERY* BODY

BOY SHORT

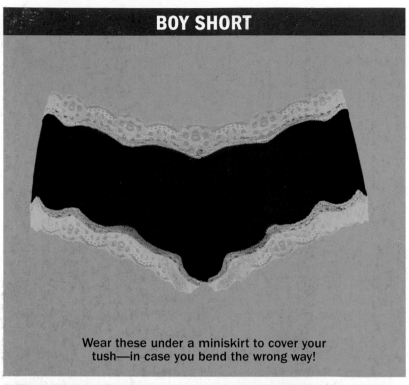

Wear these under a miniskirt to cover your tush—in case you bend the wrong way!

BIKINI

Bikini bottoms are cut higher on the leg but still give you a little butt coverage.

SEAMLESS

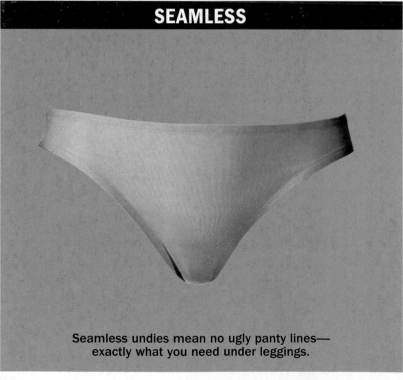

Seamless undies mean no ugly panty lines—exactly what you need under leggings.

THONG

The wide lace band means no bulkiness when you wear them with your skinniest pants.

HIPSTER

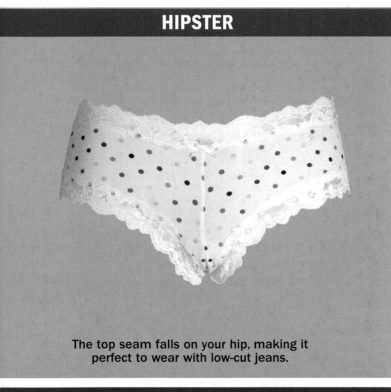

The top seam falls on your hip, making it perfect to wear with low-cut jeans.

TUMMY SHAPER

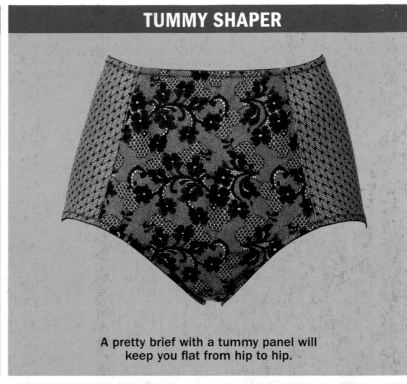

A pretty brief with a tummy panel will keep you flat from hip to hip.

THIGH SHAPER

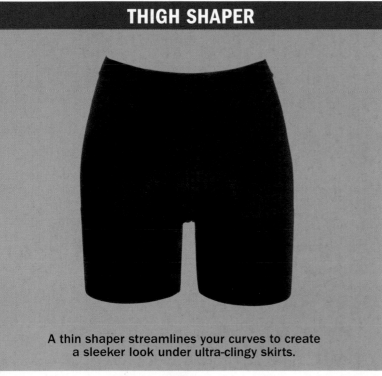

A thin shaper streamlines your curves to create a sleeker look under ultra-clingy skirts.

HIGH CUT

This extra-comfy style sits high enough on your tummy so it won't create rolls.

PHOTO CREDITS

p. 1: Nicholas Routzen. Sittings Editor: Betsy Mullinix; **p. 2:** Nicholas Routzen. Styled by Anna Levak at 1plus1management.com; **p. 4:** Juan Algarin. Styled by Mimi Lombardo; **p. 6:** Perry Hagopian. Sittings Editor: Betsy Mullinix. Hair: Johnny Lavoy, Ford Artists NYC for Kérastase. Makeup: Samantha Trinh. Manicure: Ana Maria for ArtistsbyTimothyPriano.com.

CHAPTER 1: GIRLY pp. 10–11: Model (main): Juan Algarin; Styled by Mimi Lombardo; Runway (top): Frazer Harrison/Getty Images; Heart locket: Dorling Kindersley/Getty Images; Pink rose: Rosemary Calvert/Getty Images; Blue ribbon: Tsuneo Yamashita/Getty Images; Butterfly: Digital Vision/Getty Images; Frame: George Doyle/Getty Images; Lollipop: Simon Belcher/Alamy; Tiara: Tom Schierlitz/Getty Images; "Love Ya" Candy: Tom Schierlitz/Getty Images; Ribbons and petals: Jules Frazier/Getty Images; Audrey Hepburn: Hulton Archive/Getty Images; Cupcake: Kathryn Harris/ 4Goodnesscake/Getty Images; Yellow flower: Daniel Sambraus/Getty Images; Runway (bottom left): Maria Valentino/MCV Photo; Lace (2): Thinkstock; Pink bag and green skirt: Jesus Ayala/Studio D; Styled by Christy Alcebo; Jelly beans: Aaron Graubart/Getty Images; Flower bouquet: Tobias Titz/Getty Images; Quilted fabric swatch: Dorling Kindersley/Getty Images; Pink and purple candy: Kelly Bowden/Getty Images; Sunglasses: Thinkstock; Balloons: Taesam Do/Getty Images; Photo booth photo: Design Pics/Ashley Armstrong/Getty Images; Heart cookie: Foodcollection.com/Alamy; Pearls: Davies and Starr/Getty Images; Note and heart pin: ULTRA.F/Getty Images; Heart-shaped candies: SW Productions/Getty Images; Cherry: Tom Grill/Getty Images; Butterfly (Bottom right): Stockbyte/Getty Images; Lipstick kiss: Walt Seng/Getty Images; Red ribbon: Thinkstock; Bowtie: Thinkstock; Lace (2): Thinkstock; Model (bottom, center): Brook Nipar; Sittings Editor: Betsy Mullinix; Model (right, center): Chris Eckert/Studio D; Sittings Editor: Betsy Mullinix; **pp. 12–13:** Floral Dress: Jesus Ayala/Studio D. Styled by Claire Tedaldi for Halley Resources; Ruffled Top, Boot-Cut Jeans, Cropped Cardigan, Floaty Skirt: Jesus Ayala/Studio D. Styled by Christy Alcebo; Ballet Flats: Kevin Sweeney/Studio D. Styled by Miako Katoh; Peep-Toe Heels: Charlotte Jenks Lewis/Studio D. Styled by Claire Tedaldi for Halley Resources; Soft Tee: Jesus Ayala/Studio D. Styled by Phyllis Baker; **pp. 14–15** (outfits from top to bottom): Flirty Dress Outfit: Jesus Ayala/Studio D. Styled by Claire Tedaldi for Halley Resources; Jesus Ayala/Studio D. Styled by Christy Alcebo; Courtesy of Candie's; Courtesy of Guy and Eva; Jesus Ayala/Studio D. Styled by Christy Alcebo; Ruffled Top Outfit: Jesus Ayala/Studio D. Styled by Christy Alcebo; Charlotte Jenks Lewis/Studio D. Styled by Claire Tedaldi for Halley Resources; Jesus Ayala/Studio D. Styled by Claire Tedaldi for Halley Resources; Jesus Ayala/Studio D. Styled by Christy Alcebo; Boot-cut Jeans Outfit: Jesus Ayala/Studio D. Styled by Claire Tedaldi for Halley Resources; Manictrout.com; Jesus Ayala/Studio D. Styled by Christy Alcebo (3); Cropped Cardigan Outfit: Jesus Ayala/Studio D. Styled by Claire Tedaldi for Halley Resources; Jesus Ayala/Studio D. Styled by Christy Alcebo (2); Jesus Ayala/Studio D. Styled by Claire Tedaldi for Halley Resources (2); **pp. 16–17** (outfits from top to bottom): Ballet Flats Outfit: Kevin Sweeny/Studio D. Styled By Miako Katoh; Jesus Ayala/Studio D. Styled by Claire Tedaldi for Halley Resources; Davies and Starr/Getty Images; Kevin Sweeny/Studio D. Styled By Miako Katoh; Richard Majchrzak/Studio D. Styled by Claire Tedaldi for Halley Resources; Peep-Toe Heels Outfit: Philip Friedman/Studio D; Jesus Ayala/StudioD. Styled by Claire Tedaldi for Halley Resources (2); Charlotte Jenks Lewis/Studio D. Styled by Claire Tedaldi for Halley Resources; Soft Tee Outfit: Jesus Ayala/Studio D. Styled by Phyllis Baker; Jesus Ayala/Studio D. Styled by Christy Alcebo (4); Floaty Skirt Outfit: Jesus Ayala/Studio D. Styled by Phyllis Baker; Jesus Ayala/Studio D. Styled by Miako Katoh; Jesus Ayala/StudioD. Styled by Claire Tedaldi For Halley Resources; Jesus Ayala/Studio D. Styled by Phyllis Baker; **p. 18:** Paper clip: Burazin/Getty Images; **p. 19** (Clockwise from top left): Columbia/American Zoetrope/Sony/The Kobal Collection; Jason Kempin/Getty Images; Jesus Ayala/Studio D. Styled by Claire Tedaldi for Halley Resources (2); Phil Oh; Ken Biggs/Getty Images; Philip Friedman/Studio D. Styled by Claire Tedaldi for Halley Resources; © Joan Marcus; ABC Family via Getty Images; **p. 22:** Jon Kopaloff/FilmMagic **p. 23:** GF/bauergriffinonline.com; **pp. 24–25** (left to right): BuzzFoto/Getty Images; Jon Kopaloff/FilmMagic; Rick Diamond/Getty Images; Roger Wong/INFphoto.com; Rosa/LIMELIGHTPICS.COM; Kevin Winter/Getty Images; Hot Shots Worldwide; Jackson Lee/Splash News; **pp. 26–27:** Mix Your Florals: Jesus Ayala/Studio D.; Styled by Christy Alcebo; Pile on Your Necklaces: Chris Eckert/Studio D; Sittings Editor: Betsy Mullinix; Pick the Right Cardi: Chris Eckert/Studio D; Sittings Editor: Betsy Mullinix; Accessorize Your Hair: Robert Diadul; Stylist: Danielle Nachmani; Just Add Heels: Chris Eckert/Studio D; Sittings Editor: Betsy Mullinix; Winterize Your Summer Dress: Chris Eckert/Studio D;

Sittings Editor: Betsy Mullinix **pp. 28–29:** (top row, left to right): Maria Valentino/MCV Photo; Jean Baptiste Lacroix/Getty Images; Phil Oh; Dimitrios Kambouris/WireImage; Alexander Tamargo/Getty Images; Maria Valentino/ MCV Photo; (bottom row, left to right): Mr. Newton; Antonio de Moraes Barros/WireImage; Dave M. Benett/Getty Images; Karl Prouse/Catwalking/Getty Images; Frazer Harrison/Getty Images; Missy Pasquale; Kevin Mazur/Getty Images; Maria Valentino/ MCV Photo; **pp. 30–31:** Philip Friedman/Studio D.

CHAPTER 2: EDGY pp. 32–33: Model (main): Danielle St. Laurent. Sittings Editor: Betsy Mullinix; Taylor Momsen: Startraks; Skull ring: J Muckle/Studio D; Chain necklace: Jesus Ayala/Studio D. Styled by Claire Tedaldi for Halley Resources; Graffiti: Vasiliki Varvaki/Getty Images; Splatter with chains: Phil Ashley/Getty Images; Paint splatters: Chris Stein/Getty Images; Chain links: Richard Majchrzak/Studio D. Styled by Claire Tedaldi for Halley Resources; Heart with safety pin: John Foxx/Getty Images; Leather swatch: Thinkstock; Denim zipper: Halfdark/Getty Images; Safety pin: Burazin/Getty Images; Leather jacket: Tom Schierlitz/Getty Images; Ripped denim: Bill Steele/Getty Images; Plaid change purse: CSA Plastock/Getty Images; Electric guitar: Untitled X-Ray/Nick Veasey/Getty Images; Headphones: Tom Schierlitz/Getty Images; Red plaid fabric: Arthur S. Aubry/Getty Images; Snake: Michael "Dino" Henderson/Getty images; Chain heart: PIER/Getty Images; Skateboard heart: Thinkstock; Runway: Chris Moore/Catwalking/Getty Images; Motorcycle: Fuse/Getty Images; Chain links: Richard Majchrzak/Studio D. Styled by Claire Tedaldi for Halley Resources; Zebra-print swatch: Donna Ikkanda/Getty Images; Snakeskin swatch: Siede Preis/Getty Images; Chained heart: Buena Vista Images; Drumsticks: Image Source/Getty Images; Woven leather swatch: Thinkstock; Mascara: Christopher Stevenson/Getty Images; Blue abstract: Gerard Hermand/Getty Images; Neon abstract: Jan Bruggeman/Getty Images; Leather glove: Jesus Ayala/Studio D. Styled by Claire Tedaldi for Halley Resources; *Twilight* poster: AF archive/Alamy; **pp. 34–35:** Skinny Jeans: Jesus Ayala/Studio D. Styled by Christy Alcebo; Tunic Top: Jesus Ayala/Studio D. Styled by Claire Tedaldi for Halley Resources; Leather Bomber: Jesus Ayala/Studio D. Styled by John Olson; Booties: J Muckle/Studio D. Styled by Claire Tedaldi for Halley Resources; Black Mini: Jesus Ayala/Studio D. Styled by Claire Tedaldi for Halley Resources; Denim Cutoffs: Courtesy of Siwy; Rock Tee: Jesus Ayala/Studio D. Styled by Claire Tedaldi for Halley Resources; Motorcycle Boots: Jesus Ayala/Studio D. Styled by Claire Tedaldi for Halley Resources **pp. 36–37** (outfits from top to bottom): Skinny Jeans Outfit: Jesus Ayala/Studio D. Styled by Claire Tedaldi for Halley Resources; Courtesy of Lulu's; Jesus Ayala/Studio D. Styled by Christy Alcebo; Jesus Ayala/Studio D. Styled by Phyllis Baker; Courtesy Of Nine West; Rock Tee Outfit: Jesus Ayala/Studio D. Styled by Christy Alcebo; Jesus Ayala/Studio D. Styled by Claire Tedaldi for Halley Resources (2); Jesus Ayala/Studio D. Styled by Christy Alcebo; Booties Outfit: Jesus Ayala/Studio D. Styled by Christy Alcebo; Jesus Ayala/Studio D. Styled by Claire Tedaldi for Halley Resources; J Muckle/Studio D; Jesus Ayala/Studio D. Styled by Phyllis Baker; J Muckle/Studio D. Styled by Claire Tedaldi for Halley Resources; Tunic Top Outfit: Jesus Ayala/Studio D. Styled by Claire Tedaldi for Halley Resources; Jesus Ayala/Studio D. Styled by Christy Alcebo; Jesus Ayala/Studio D. Styled by Christy Alcebo; Philip Friedman/Studio D; Courtesy of AMI Clubwear; **pp. 38–39** (outfits from top to bottom): Leather Bomber Outfit: Jesus Ayala/Studio D. Styled by Claire Tedaldi for Halley Resources; Jesus Ayala/Studio D. Styled by John Olson; Philip Friedman/Studio D. Styled by Miako Katoh; Jesus Ayala/Studio D. Styled by Claire Tedaldi for Halley Resources (2); Black Mini Outfit: Jesus Ayala/Studio D. Styled by Claire Tedaldi for Halley Resources (4); Jesus Ayala/Studio D; Denim Cutoffs Outfit: Richard Majchrzak/Studio D. Styled by Phyllis Baker; Jesus Ayala/Studio D. Styled by Christy Alcebo; David Lewis Taylor/Studio D. Styled by Christy Alcebo; J Muckle/Studio D; Charlotte Jenks Lewis/Studio D. Styled by Claire Tedaldi for Halley Resources; Jesus Ayala/Studio D. Styled by Claire Tedaldi for Halley Resources; Motorcycle Boots Outfit: Jesus Ayala/Studio D. Styled by Christy Alcebo; Jesus Ayala/Studio D. Styled by Phyllis Baker; Jesus Ayala/Studio D. Styled by Claire Tedaldi for Halley Resources; Christopher Coppola/Studio D. Styled by John Olson; **p. 40:** Paper clip: Burazin/Getty Images; **p. 41** (clockwise from top left): Jesus Ayala/Studio D. Styled by Claire Tedaldi for Halley Resources; J Muckle/Studio D; AFP/Getty Images; Iain Masterton/Getty Images; Getty Images; Gabriela Maj/Getty Images; Kevin Sweeney/Studio D. Styled by Karen Larrain; Richard Majchrzak/Studio D. Styled by Claire Tedaldi for Halley Resources; J Muckle/Studio D; Soul Brother/FilmMagic; **p. 44:** Steve Granitz/Wireimage; **p. 45:** Jason LaVeris/FilmMagic **pp. 46–47** (left to right): Startraks; Jon Kopaloff/FilmMagic; Startraks (2); Steve Granitz/WireImage; Florian Seefried/Getty Images; Startraks; Jean Baptiste Lacroix/WireImage **pp. 48–49:** Step Up Your Sweats: Nicholas Routzen. Styled by Kristin

Studio D. Styled by Yolande Gagnier; Cuff Your Skinnies: Nicholas Routzen. Sittings Editor: Betsy Mullinix; Mix Posh and Sporty: Styled by Anna Levak at 1plus1management.com; Make Sexy More Subtle: Anna Wolf. Sittings Editor: Betsy Mullinix. **pp. 94–95:** (top row, left to right): Ashley Barrett. Sittings Editor: Betsy Mullinix; INFphoto.com; Maria Valentino/ MCV Photo; Splash News; JP Yim/WireImage; Frazer Harrison/Getty Images; (bottom row, left to right): John Shearer/Getty Images; Startraks; Missy Pasquale; Dominique Charriau/WireImage; Mr. Newton; Startraks; Getty Images for IMG; Missy Pasquale; **pp. 96–97:** Philip Friedman/Studio D.

CHAPTER 5: GLAM **pp. 98–99:** Model (main): Terry Doyle. Styled by Elise Wilson at Ray Brown Pro; Star earrings: Jesus Ayala/Studio D. Styled by Christina Hurley-Scott; Beyoncé: (Kevin Mazur/WireImage) Red glitter border: (Handypix/Alamy); Rings: James Worrell/Getty Images; Sparkling star: Jesus Ayala/Studio D. Styled by Claire Tedaldi for Halley Resources; Gold glitter swatch: *adrisbow* (adriana lopetrone); Clutch: Jay Muckle/Studio D. Styled by Christy Alcebo; Jewels: Jesus Ayala/Studio D. Styled by Claire Tedaldi for Halley Resources; Rhinestones: Tooga/Getty Images; Disco ball: Buena Vista Images; Purple glitter swatch: Cooter/Alamy; Feather boa: Steve Gorton/Getty Images; Star wand: Richard Brown/Getty Images; Chandelier earring: Jesus Ayala/Studio D. Styled by Claire Tedaldi for Halley Resources; Marilyn Monroe Hollywood star: Randy Wells/Getty Images; Marilyn Monroe by Andy Warhol: AFP/Getty Images; Blue sequined fabric: Thinkstock; Hollywood sign: Tim Hawley/Getty Images; Purple lipstick: Stuart Tyson/Studio D; Leopard print swatch: Thinkstock; Gold border: (Oliver Leedham/Alamy); Lip print: Walt Seng/Getty Images; Diamond: Ryan McVay/Getty Images; Pink feather: Steve Shott/Getty Images; Silver glitter swatch: Aaron Cobbett/Getty Images; Red heels: Tom Schierlitz/Getty Images; Lashes: J Muckle/Studio D; Star confetti: Thinkstock; Runway: Antonio de Moraes Barros/Getty Images; Lady Gaga: Kevin Mazur/Getty Images; Sunglasses: Kevin Sweeney/Studio D; **pp. 100–101:** Sparkly Dress: Jesus Ayala/Studio D. Styled by Claire Tedaldi for Halley Resources; Dark Skinnies: Jesus Ayala/Studio D. Styled by Claire Tedaldi for Halley Resources; Fur Vest: Jesus Ayala/Studio D. Styled by Claire Tedaldi for Halley Resources; Leopard-Print Top: Jesus Ayala/Studio D. Styled by Claire Tedaldi for Halley Resources; Romper: Philip Friedman/Studio D. Styled by Claire Tedaldi for Halley Resources; Platform Heels: Jesus Ayala/Studio D. Styled by Claire Tedaldi for Halley Resources; Pencil Skirt: Jesus Ayala/Studio D. Styled by Claire Tedaldi for Halley Resources; High-Heel Boot: Philip Friedman/Studio D. Styled by Claire Tedaldi for Halley Resources; **pp. 102–103** (outfits from top to bottom): Sparkly Dress Outfit: Jesus Ayala/Studio D. Styled by Claire Tedaldi for Halley Resources; Jesus Ayala/Studio D. Styled by Christy Alcebo; Courtesy of DSW; Jesus Ayala/Studio D. Styled By John Olson; Dark Skinnies Outfit: J Muckle/Studio D. Styled by Claire Tedaldi for Halley Resources; Jesus Ayala/Studio D. Styled by Claire Tedaldi for Halley Resources; Jesus Ayala/Studio D. Styled by Christy Alcebo; Jesus Ayala/Studio D. Styled by Claire Tedaldi for Halley Resources (2); Leopard-Print Top Outfit: Jesus Ayala/Studio D. Styled by Claire Tedaldi for Halley Resources; Courtesy of Candies; Philip Friedman/Studio D. Styled by Miako Katoh; Jesus Ayala/Studio D. Styled by Christy Alcebo; Kevin Sweeney/Studio D. Styled by Miako Katoh; Platform Heels Outfit: Jesus Ayala/Studio D. Styled by Claire Tedaldi for Halley Resources (5); **pp. 104–105** (outfits from top to bottom): Pencil Skirt Outfit: Jesus Ayala/Studio D. Styled by Christy Alcebo; Jesus Ayala/Studio D. Styled by Claire Tedaldi for Halley Resources; Jesus Ayala/Studio D. Styled by Christy Alcebo; Jesus Ayala/Studio D. Styled by Claire Tedaldi for Halley Resources; Courtesy of Carrie Valentine; Jesus Ayala/Studio D. Styled by Claire Tedaldi for Halley Resources; Fur Vest Outfit: Jesus Ayala/Studio D. Styled by Christy Alcebo; Jesus Ayala/Studio D. Styled by Claire Tedaldi for Halley Resources (3); Romper Outfit: Philip Friedman/Studio D. Styled by by Claire Tedaldi for Halley Resources; Jesus Ayala/Studio D. Styled by Christy Alcebo; Jesus Ayala/Studio D. Styled by Claire Tedaldi for Halley Resources; Jesus Ayala/Studio D. Styled by Christy Alcebo; Jesus Ayala/Studio D. Styled by Claire Tedaldi for Halley Resources; High-Heel Boots Outfit: Jesus Ayala/Studio D. Styled by Claire Tedaldi for Halley Resources; Jesus Ayala/Studio D. Styled by Christy Alcebo (2); Christopher Coppola/Studio D. Styled by John Olsen; Philip Friedman/Studio D. Styled by Claire Tedaldi for Halley Resources; **p. 106:** Paper clip: Burazin/Getty Images; **p. 107** (clockwise from from top left): Kristian Dowling/Getty Images; Karl Prouse/Catwalking; Antonio de Moraes Barros/WireImage; 20th Century Fox/The Kobal Collection (2); Light Thru My Lens Photography/Getty Images; Courtesy of Guerlain; Jesus Ayala/Studio D. Styled by Claire Tedaldi for Halley Resources (4); Arnaldo Magnani/Getty Images; **p. 110:** Jeff Kravitz/AMA2010/FilmMagic; **p. 111:** Shareif Ziyadat/FilmMagic; **pp. 112–113** (left to right): Jemal Countess/WireImage; Michael Tran/FilmMagic; Jackson Lee / Splash News; Chung Sung-Jun/Getty Images; Gotcha Images/Splash News; Eric Ryan/Getty Images; Dave M. Benett/Getty Images;

Startraks; **pp. 114–115:** Wear Sparkle at School: Jesus Ayala/Studio D. Styled by John Olson; Go Big or Go Home: Danielle St. Laurent. Sittings Editor: Betsy Mullinix; Nail Your Look: Wendy Hope/Studio D. Fashion Stylist: Jasmine Snow; Flirt with Fur: Marley Kate; Sittings Editor: Betsy Mullinix; Slip into Shiny Shorts: Juan Algarin. Styled by Mimi Lombardo; Bust Out the Bustier: Nicholas Routzen. Sittings Editor: Betsy Mullinix; **pp. 116–117:** (top row, left to right): Maria Valentino/MCV Photo; Mike Coppola/Getty Images; JP Yim/WireImage; Startraks; Missy Pasquale; Mike Marsland/WireImage; (bottom row, left to right): Venturelli/WireImage; Jon Kopaloff/FilmMagic; Frazer Harrison/Getty Images; Maria Valentino/MCV Photo; David Livingston/Getty Images; Antonio de Moraes Barros/WireImage; Mr. Newton; Venturelli/WireImage; **pp. 118–119:** Philip Friedman/Studio D.

CHAPTER 6: INDIE **pp. 120–121:** Model (main): Sarra Fleur Abou-El-Haj/Studio D. Sittings Editor: Betsy Mullinix; Scarf: Jesus Ayala/Studio D. Styled by Claire Tedaldi For Halley Resources; Russian doll: Stockbyte/Getty Images; Runway: JP Yim/Getty Images; Buttons (2): Philip Friedman/Studio D; Mondrian painting: DEA PICTURE LIBRARY; Sock monkey: Andy Crawford/Getty Images; Colored pencils: George Doyle/Getty Images; Gem necklace: Gerry Charm/Getty Images; Vintage poster: Barbara Singer/Getty Images; Sushi: Diane Macdonald/Getty Images; Camera: Creative Crop; Shoe sketch: Mo Ulicny/Getty Images; Rothko Painting: AFP/Getty Images; Orange blossom: Lauren Burke/Getty Images; iPod with headphones: Philip Friedman/Studio D; Skateboard: Thinkstock; Buttons (2): Peter Anderson/Getty Images; Key: Getty Images; Notepad sketch: Alex Stsiazhyn/Getty Images; Buttons (4): sot/Getty Images; Tragedy and comedy masks: Ian McKinnell/Getty Images; Photo album: Richard Goerg/Getty Images; Hummingbird: Cyril Laubscher/Getty Images; Notebook and pencil: Dave King/Getty Images; Katy Perry: Jesal Parshotam, PacificCoastNews.com; Paintbrushes: Fuse/Getty Images; Butterfly print: Circa/Getty Images; Fedora: Jesus Ayala/Studio D. Styled by Claire Tedaldi For Halley Resources; Buttons (3) Peter Anderson/Getty Images; Checker pattern swatch: Rian Hughes/Getty Images; **pp. 122–123:** High-Waisted Jeans, Retro Dress: Jesus Ayala/Studio D Styled by Christy Alcebo; All Others: Jesus Ayala/Studio D. Styled by Claire Tedaldi for Halley Resources; **pp. 124–125** (outfits from top to bottom): High-Waisted Jeans Outfit: Jesus Ayala/Studio D. Styled by Christy Alcebo (2); Jesus Ayala/Studio D. Styled by Claire Tedaldi for Halley Resources; Jesus Ayala/Studio D Styled by Christy Alcebo (2); Drapey Cardigan Outfit: Jesus Ayala/Studio D. Styled by Claire Tedaldi for Halley Resources (3); Crewneck Sweatshirt Outfit: Jesus Ayala/Studio D. Styled by Phyllis Baker; Jesus Ayala/Studio D. Styled by Claire Tedaldi for Halley Resources; David Turner/Studio D. Styled by Tricia Biancamano; Jesus Ayala/Studio D. Styled by Claire Tedaldi for Halley Resources (2); Jesus Ayala/Studio D. Styled by Phyllis Baker; Oxford Shoes Outfit: Jesus Ayala/Studio D. Styled by Claire Tedaldi for Halley Resources (3): **pp. 126–127** (outfits from top to bottom): Shorts Outfit: Jesus Ayala/Studio D. Styled by Phyllis Baker; Jesus Ayala/Studio D. Styled by Christy Alcebo; Jesus Ayala/Studio D. Styled by Miako Katoh; Jesus Ayala/Studio D. Styled by Christy Alcebo; Jesus Ayala/Studio D. Styled by Christy Alcebo; Wedge Boots Outfit: Jesus Ayala/Studio D. Styled by Claire Tedaldi for Halley Resources (2); Jesus Ayala/Studio D. Styled by Miako Katoh; Jesus Ayala/Studio D. Styled by Phyllis Baker; Jesus Ayala/Studio D. Styled by Claire Tedaldi for Halley Resources; Plaid Shirt Outfit: Jesus Ayala/Studio D. Styled by Claire Tedaldi for Halley Resources; Jesus Ayala/Studio D. Styled by Phyllis Baker; Jesus Ayala/Studio D. Styled by Claire Tedaldi for Halley Resources; Jesus Ayala/Studio D. Styled by Christy Alcebo; Kevin Sweeney/Studio D. Styled Miako Katoh; Retro Dress Outfit: Jesus Ayala/Studio D. Styled by Christy Alcebo (4); **p. 128:** Paper clip: Burazin/Getty Images; **p. 129** (clockwise from top left): Maria Valentino/MCV Photo (2); Chris Moore/Catwalking; Redferns/Getty Images Jesus Ayala/Studio D. Styled by Phyllis Baker; Chrysalis Records/Getty Images; Michael Ochs Archives/Getty Images; Walt Disney Pictures/ The Kobal Collection; Christopher Coppola/Studio D. Styled by John Olson; **p. 132:** Getty Images; **p. 133:** Jim Spellman/WireImage; **pp. 132–132** (left to right): XPOSUREPHOTOS.COM; Ian West/Press Association Images/ABACAUSA.COM; Mike Marsland/WireImage; Fred Duval/FilmMagic; Startraks; Flynet; Bauger-Griffin/Eroteme.co.uk; TSEL/Splash News; **pp. 136–137:** Try Bright Legwear: Sarra Fleur Abou-El-Haj/StudioD. Sittings Editor: Betsy Mullinix; Draw on Everything: Chris Eckert/Studio D. Sittings Editor: Betsy Mullinix; Tie on a Scarf: Chris Eckert/Studio D. Sittings Editor: Betsy Mullinix; Mix Up Your Patterns: Mei Tao. Sittings Editor: Betsy Mullinix; Play with Proportions: Terry Doyle. Styled by Turner and Erica; Wear Socks with Sandals: Chris Eckert/Studio D. Sittings Editor: Betsy Mullinix; **pp. 138–139** (top row, left to right): Startraks; Courtesy of Lydia/styleisstyle.blogspot.com; Mr. Newton; Maria Valentino/ MCV Photo; Rabbani and Solimene/WireImage; Colette DeBarros. Styled by Beau Quillian; (bottom row, left to right): Maria Valentino/ MCV Photo; Dr. Billy Ingram/WireImage; JP Yim/WireImage; Missy Pasquale; Chris Moore/Catwalking/Getty

Images; Hugh Dillon/WENN.com; Chris Moore/Catwalking/Getty Images; Startraks; **pp. 140–141:** Philip Friedman/Studio D.

YOUR ULTIMATE ACCESSORY GUIDE pp. 144–145:

Flats: Jesus Ayala/Studio D. Styled by Claire Tedaldi for Halley Resources; Heels: Jesus Ayala/Studio D. Styled by Christy Alcebo; Oxfords: Kevin Sweeney/Studio D. Styled by Christy Alcebo; Sneakers: Jesus Ayala/Studio D. Styled by Christy Alcebo; Wedges: Jesus Ayala/Studio D. Styled by Claire Tedaldi for Halley Resources; Boat Shoes: Jesus Ayala/Studio D. Styled by Claire Tedaldi for Halley Resources; Moto Boots: Jesus Ayala/Studio D. Styled by Christy Alcebo; Sandals: Jesus Ayala/Studio D. Styled by Claire Tedaldi for Halley Resources; High-Tops: Jesus Ayala/Studio D. Styled by Phyllis Baker; **pp. 146–147:** Hobo: Jesus Ayala/Studio D. Styled by Claire Tedaldi for Halley Resources; Shoulder: Jesus Ayala/Studio D. Styled by Christy Alcebo; Clutch: Jesus Ayala/Studio D. Styled by Christy Alcebo; Cross-Body: Richard Majchrzak/Studio D. Styled by Claire Tedaldi for Halley Resources; Backpack: Jesus Ayala/Studio D. Styled by Claire Tedaldi for Halley Resources; Tote: Jesus Ayala/Studio D. Styled by Phyllis Baker; Messenger: Jesus Ayala/Studio D. Styled by Phyllis Baker; Short-Handled: Jesus Ayala/Studio D. Styled by Claire Tedaldi for Halley Resources; **pp. 148–149:** Rings (left to right): Jesus Ayala/Studio D. Styled by Claire Tedaldi for Halley Resources; Philip Friedman/Studio D; Marko Metzinger/Studio D; Bracelets (left to right): Jesus Ayala/Studio D. Styled by Phyllis Baker; Charlotte Jenks Lewis/Studio D. Styled by Kristy Vant at Mark Edward Inc; Jesus Ayala/Studio D. Styled by Christy Alcebo; Necklaces (left to right): Jesus Ayala/Studio D. Styled by Christy Alcebo; Philip Friedman/Studio D. Styled by Miako Katoh; Kevin Sweeney/Studio D. Styled by Miako Katoh; Earrings (left to right): Jesus Ayala/Studio D. Styled by Christy Alcebo; Lara Robby/Studio D; Philip Friedman/Studio D. Styled by Miako Katoh; **pp. 150–151:** Cap: Jesus Ayala/Studio D. Styled by Christy Alcebo; Bucket: Jesus Ayala/Studio D. Styled by Christy Alcebo; Bomber: Philip Friedman/Studio D; Beanie: Kevin Sweeney/Studio D. Styled by Miako Katoh; Military: Jesus Ayala/Studio D. Styled by Claire Tedaldi for Halley Resources; Fedora: Jesus Ayala/Studio D. Styled by Claire Tedaldi for Halley Resources; Knit: Philip Friedman/Studio D; Newsboy: Jesus Ayala/Studio D. Styled by Phyllis Baker; Beret: Jesus Ayala/Studio D. Styled by Claire Tedaldi for Halley Resources; **pp. 152–153:** Oversize: Jesus Ayala/Studio D. Styled by Claire Tedaldi for Halley Resources; Square: Jesus Ayala/Studio D. Styled by Claire Tedaldi for Halley Resources; Aviator: Jesus Ayala/Studio D; Round: Jesus Ayala/Studio D. Styled by Claire Tedaldi for Halley Resources; Cat's Eye: Jesus Ayala/Studio D. Styled by Claire Tedaldi for Halley Resources; Novelty: Achim Sass/Getty Images; Wraparound: Jesus Ayala/Studio D. Styled by Phyllis Baker; Wayfarer: Jesus Ayala/Studio D. Styled by Miako Katoh; **pp. 154–155:** Tights: Jesus Ayala/Studio D. Styled by Claire Tedaldi for Halley Resources; Socks (left to right): Jesus Ayala/Studio D. Styled by Christy Alcebo; Christopher Coppola/Studio D. Styled by John Olson; Scarves (left to right): Jesus Ayala/Studio D. Styled by Claire Tedaldi for Halley Resources; Marko Metzinger/Studio D. Styled by Anita Salerno for R.J. Bennett Represents; Jesus Ayala/Studio D. Styled by Claire Tedaldi for Halley Resources; Hair Accessories (top to bottom): Feather Headband: Charlotte Jenks Lewis/Studio D. Styled by Claire Tedaldi for Halley Resources; Thin Headbands: Don Penny/Studio D; J Muckle/Studio D (4); Clips from left to right): J Muckle/Studio D (3); Jesus Ayala/Studio D; Belts (top to bottom): Jesus Ayala/Studio D. Styled by Christy Alcebo; Jesus Ayala/Studio D. Styled by Claire Tedaldi for Halley Resources; **p. 156** (clockwise from top left): Jesus Ayala/Studio D. Styled by Claire Tedaldi for Halley Resources (2); Richard Majchrzak/Studio D. Styled by Phyllis Baker; Jesus Ayala/Studio D. Styled by Christy Alcebo (2); Christopher Coppola/Studio D; Jesus Ayala/Studio D. Styled by Claire Tedaldi for Halley Resources; J Muckle/Studio D. Styled by Claire Tedaldi for Halley Resources; Jesus Ayala/Studio D. Styled by Claire Tedaldi for Halley Resources; Don Penny/Studio D; **p. 157** (clockwise from top left): Jesus Ayala/Studio D. Styled by Claire Tedaldi for Halley Resource (7); Philip Friedman/Studio D. Styled by Miako Katoh; **p. 158** (clockwise from top left): Jesus Ayala/Studio D. Styled by Phyllis Baker; Jesus Ayala/Studio D. Styled by Christy Alcebo (2); Jesus Ayala/Studio D. Styled by Claire Tedaldi for Halley Resources (3); Jesus Ayala/Studio D. Styled by Christy Alcebo; J Muckle/Studio D; **p. 159** (clockwise from top left): Friedman/Studio D. Styled by Miako Katoh; J Muckle/Studio D; Jesus Ayala/Studio D. Styled by Miako Katoh; Jesus Ayala/Studio D. Styled by Claire Tedaldi for Halley Resources; Jesus Ayala/Studio D. Styled by Phyllis Baker; Jesus Ayala/Studio D. Styled by Christy Alcebo; Jesus Ayala/Studio D. Styled by Claire Tedaldi for Halley Resources; Jesus Ayala/Studio D. Styled by Miako Katoh; **p. 160:** (clockwise from top left): Jesus Ayala/Studio D. Styled by Claire Tedaldi for Halley Resources (3); Jesus Ayala/Studio D. Styled by Christy Alcebo; Philip Friedman/Studio D. Styled by Tricia Biancamano; Jesus Ayala/Studio D. Styled by Claire Tedaldi for Halley Resources (2); Marko Metzinger/Studio D;

p. 161 (clockwise from top left): Jesus Ayala/Studio D. Styled by Christy Alcebo; Jesus Ayala/Studio D. Styled by Claire Tedaldi for Halley Resources; Jesus Ayala/Studio D. Styled by Phyllis Baker; Jesus Ayala/Studio D. Styled by Claire Tedaldi for Halley Resources (2); Courtesy of Betsey Johnson; Jesus Ayala/Studio D. Styled by Claire Tedaldi for Halley Resources (2).

YOUR ULTIMATE FIT GUIDE pp. 164–165: Denim background: dmitry@mordolff.ru; Models: Robert Diadul. Styled by Anna Levak at 1plus-1management.com; **pp. 166–167** (left to right): Shannon Sinclair. Sittings Editor: Betsy Mullinix (2). Chris Eckert/Studio D. Sittings Editor: Betsy Mullinix (2); **pp. 168–169** (left to right): Chris Eckert/Studio D. Sittings Editor: Betsy Mullinix; Shannon Sinclair. Sittings Editor: Betsy Mullinix (2); Chris Eckert/Studio D. Sittings Editor: Betsy Mullinix; **pp. 170–171** (columns from left to right, top to bottom): Curvy All Over: Jesus Ayala/Studio D. Styled by Claire Tedaldi for Halley Resources; Jesus Ayala/Studio D. Styled by Christy Alcebo; Jesus Ayala/Studio D. Styled by Claire Tedaldi for Halley Resources; Tall: Jesus Ayala/Studio D. Styled by Claire Tedaldi for Halley Resources (3); Curvy Butt: Jesus Ayala/Studio D. Styled by Christy Alcebo (3); Curvy Tummy: Jesus Ayala/Studio D. Styled by Christy Alcebo (3); Flat Butt: Jesus Ayala/Studio D. Styled by Christy Alcebo (3); Curvy Thighs: Jesus Ayala/Studio D. Styled by Christy Alcebo (2); Jesus Ayala/Studio D. Styled by Claire Tedaldi for Halley Resources; Petite: Jesus Ayala/Studio D. Styled by Claire Tedaldi for Halley Resources (2); Jesus Ayala/Studio D. Styled by Christy Alcebo; Curvy Hips: Jesus Ayala/Studio D. Styled by Claire Tedaldi for Halley Resources; Jesus Ayala/Studio D. Styled by Christy Alcebo (2); **pp. 172–173:** Water background: Yasinguneysu/Getty Images; Models: Jason Todd; **pp. 174–175** (left to right): Danielle St. Laurent. Sittings Editor: Betsy Mullinix; Beth Studenberg. Styled by Annebet Duvall; Chris Eckert. Sittings Editor: Betsy Mullinix; Danielle St. Laurent. Sittings Editor: Betsy Mullinix; **pp. 176–177** (left to right): Beth Studenberg. Styled by Annebet Duvall; Danielle St. Laurent. Sittings Editor: Betsy Mullinix (2); Beth Studenberg. Styled by Annebet Duvall; **pp. 178–179** (columns from left to right, top to bottom): Small Bust: Jesus Ayala/Studio D. Styled by Claire Tedaldi for Halley Resources; Jesus Ayala/Studio D. Styled by Christy Alcebo (2); Boyish: Jesus Ayala/Studio D. Styled by Claire Tedaldi for Halley Resources; Courtesy of Aéropostale; Jesus Ayala/Studio D. Styled by Christy Alcebo; Curvy Butt: Jesus Ayala/Studio D. Styled by Christy Alcebo; Jesus Ayala/Studio D. Styled by Claire Tedaldi for Halley Resources (2); Curvy All Over: Jesus Ayala/Studio D. Styled by Miako Katoh; Jesus Ayala/Studio D. Styled by Claire Tedaldi for Halley Resources; Jesus Ayala/Studio D. Styled by Miako Katoh; Full Bust: Jesus Ayala/Studio D. Styled by Miako Katoh ; Jesus Ayala/Studio D. Styled by Claire Tedaldi for Halley Resources (2); Curvy Hips: Jesus Ayala/Studio D. Styled by Miako Katoh; Jesus Ayala/Studio D. Styled by Christy Alcebo; Jesus Ayala/Studio D. Styled by Miako Katoh; Flat Butt: J Muckle/Studio D. Styled by Christina Hurley; Jesus Ayala/Studio D. Styled by Christy Alcebo; Jesus Ayala/Studio D. Styled by Miako Katoh; Curvy Tummy: Jesus Ayala/Studio D. Styled by Christy Alcebo; Jesus Ayala/Studio D. Styled by Miako Katoh; Courtesy of Crystal Jin; **pp. 180–181:** Lace background: Thinkstock; Models: Jason Todd; **pp. 182–183:** Models: Anna Palma. Styled by Kristin Rawson at See Management; Bras: Jesus Ayala/Studio D. Styled by Claire Tedaldi for Halley Resources; **pp. 184–185:** Models: Anna Palma. Styled by Kristin Rawson at See Management; Bras: Jesus Ayala/Studio D. Styled by Claire Tedaldi for Halley Resources; **pp. 186–187:** Boyshort, Bikini, Thong, and Hipster: Jesus Ayala /Studio D. Styled by Claire Tedaldi for Halley Resources; Tummy Shaper, Thigh Shaper, Seamless, and High-Cut: Jesus Ayala/Studio D. Styled by Christy Alcebo.

REAL GIRL PHOTO CREDITS

Girly (Shalyn), Edgy (Nicole), Classic (Daisy), Glam (Remy), Indie (Stephanie):
Photographer: Chris Eckert/Studio D
Art Director: Miranda Sheppard
Stylist: Betsy Mullinix
Hair: Tyler Laswell for TRESemmé/contactnyc.com
Makeup: Thora @ Kate Ryan Inc. for Benefit Cosmetics
Manicure: Tatyana Molot at ArtistsbyTimothyPriano.com

Boho (Andie):
Photographer: Sarra Fleur Abou-El-Haj/Studio D
Art Director: Miranda Sheppard
Stylist: Jasmine Snow
Hair: Tyler Laswell for TRESemmé/contactnyc.com
Makeup: Claudia Lake for NARS Cosmetics/contactnyc
Manicure: Sue Nam at ArtistsbyTimothyPriano.com

THIS BOOK WAS PRODUCED BY

 MELCHER
MEDIA

124 West 13th Street
New York, NY 10011
www.melcher.com

PRESIDENT AND PUBLISHER **CHARLES MELCHER**
ASSOCIATE PUBLISHER **BONNIE ELDON**
EDITOR IN CHIEF **DUNCAN BOCK**
EXECUTIVE EDITOR AND PROJECT MANAGER **LIA RONNEN**
EDITOR **MEGAN WORMAN**
PRODUCTION DIRECTOR **KURT ANDREWS**
PRODUCTION COORDINATOR **DANIEL DEL VALLE**

DESIGNED BY **NUMBER SEVENTEEN, NYC**

TEXT BY **LAUREN A. GREENE** AND **LAUREN METZ**

PHOTO EDITOR **JOSLYN B. WINKFIELD**

MARKET EDITOR **MARISSA GRUMER**

SEVENTEEN THANK-YOUS
Joanna Saltz, Jessica Musumeci, Alison Jurado, Gina Kelly,
Marissa Grumer, Joslyn Winkfield, Lauren Greene, Lauren Metz, Sally Abbey,
Betsy Mullinix, Jasmine Snow, Marisa Carroll, and Jacqueline Deval

Chris Navratil, Craig Herman, Cindy De La Hoz, and the entire Running Press team
Bonnie Siegler, Jessica Zadnik, and Lionel Cipriano at Number Seventeen
Lia Ronnen, Megan Worman, and the entire Melcher Media team

MELCHER MEDIA THANK-YOUS
David E. Brown, Róisín Cameron, Cheryl Della Pietra, Jeff Elkins,
Meghan Day Healey, Heather L. Hughes, Lauren Nathan, Austin O'Malley,
Katherine Raymond, Holly Rothman, Julia Sourikoff, and Shoshana Thaler